GATHER TOGETHER IN MY NAME

Arturo Paoli

GATHER TOGETHER IN MY NAME

Reflections on Christianity and Community

Translated from the Italian by
Robert R. Barr

ORBIS BOOKS
Maryknoll, New York 10545

BV
4501.2
.P323513
1987

The Catholic Foreign Mission Society of America (Maryknoll) recruits and trains people for overseas missionary service. Through Orbis Books Maryknoll aims to foster the international dialogue that is essential to mission. The books published, however, reflect the opinions of their authors and are not meant to represent the official position of the society.

First published as *Il presente non basta a nessuno*, 2nd ed., copyright © 1978 Cittadella Editrice, Assisi, Italy

English translation copyright © 1987 by Orbis Books, Maryknoll, NY 10545
All rights reserved
Manufactured in the United States of America
Manuscript editor: William E. Jerman

Library of Congress Cataloging-in-Publication Data

Paoli, Arturo.
   Gather together in my name.

   Translation of 2nd ed. of: Il presente non basta a nessuno.
   1. Christian life—1960-   . 2. Christianity—
20th century.   3. Liberation theology.   I. Title.
BV4501.2.P323513   1987   209′.04   86-23806
ISBN 0-88344-357-0 (pbk.)

To members of the community of Bojó,
in the west of Venezuela,
who have taught me so many things
without realizing it
and **because** *they didn't realize it.*

Contents

1

A Christian: Someone
with an Open Door

The mist between here and the hills could make me think I'm in Lombardy. But I'm in a remote area of the state of Lara, in the west of Venezuela. I can barely make out Julio and his stubborn oxen at the bottom of the hill my clay hut sits on. Julio is brandishing his goad, and the oxen are making some headway with a heavy plow in the muddy earth soaked by three days of solid rain. There is no time to lose. The *guajales*—the Canadian seed potatoes heaped up in the common store—will rot unless they're planted quickly now, rain or shine. The mist makes my solitude more solitary still, and the silence more absolute.

Pedro is in the fields hastily sowing potato chunks in the intervals granted by the rain. Twenty years old, scion of the people, he has recently had the intuition that Christ can give his life new savor. He is now my roommate. During the hours we spend together, I answer his questions and help him familiarize himself with Christian nomenclature. What is the Mass? What is the Angelus? Who is the pope? What is chastity? I ask the Holy Spirit to help me not to have him renounce his social class and not to clericalize him.

I love it when he reaches for his guitar, and, with all the power of his tropical blood, all the simple eloquence of the plainsman, sings:

1

Soy hermano de la espuma,
De la garza, de la rosa, y del sol.

Brother to the seafoam, I,
And to the crane, the rose, and the sun.

I learn something, too, when I see him reeling under a load of *guajales* with his brothers in the fields, all sinking their arms and legs into the earth, their earth. I realize that *I'm* the one learning a new "vocabulary." I have to redo the Christian vocabulary, break free from abstract learning. Forced to rediscover the Christian values of an existence stripped of any veneer, Christianity undressed, I have sudden flashes of insight into the possibility of finally practicing true poverty.

Last night Pedro ran into the word "heretic" and asked me what it meant. That really put it to me, because I realized I had to go into an ideology for that one—introduce Pedro to an alien culture. And I realized my total lack of preparation—which consisted in being too well prepared, too well trained. I felt as if he were asking me to take him by the hand, and I wanted to—all the affection I had for him made me want to—but I had my hands full. Where was I to put everything? Where could I put all my wealth?

All of those precious things I so trust in—trusting in myself—now prevent me from grasping the hand of someone who lives with me, and of millions of others besides—the ones in whose midst I live, and whose lifestyle I seek to assume, in the poverty of my hut, in my food, in my clothing. . . . Could a Pharisee perhaps be living here in this hut, where the frigid wind of the Andes comes in so easily through the holes and cracks beyond repair—someone encrusted with riches that Jesus cannot manage to scratch off him because they've become part of his skin? The ordinary wealthy are always distinct from their wealth. They can get rid of it any time they want. Pharisees are rich in their *being*. Pharisees don't *have* wealth, they *are* wealth.

Of course I could explain to Pedro what a heretic is. Perfectly well. I could explain who Luther was, who Calvin was, I could explain the denial of the Eucharist and the denial of the virginity of Mary. But he was always stopping me cold with one of those disarming questions of his. (What does the word "chastity" mean?)

The residents of our village are scarcely destitute. The valley was selected by technologists to supply the national demand for potatoes. The government, swimming in income from petroleum exports, is not terribly concerned with the cost of production here. The country folk watch the big semis roll into the huge warehouse and discharge their immense cargos of *guajales* and fertilizers. The boxes and plastic bags have foreign names on them—Canada, the U.S.A.

Everyone in the valley tries to get a bigger allotment of seed potatoes, get the sprouts into the ground, spread the fertilizer in good time, spray the young plants with insecticides, bring in the harvest at the right time, pour the potatoes into sacks, pile the sacks onto trucks—and ride down to the bank to pick up the money. Down in this clean, green, smogless valley, an assembly line is in operation.

The human being is a more and more expendable link in the chain of plans laid and launched in Caracas. The agricultural experts and the economists have worked out a potato-production plan, and have made a commitment to the government not to fall short of the necessary quotas of this staple. I can't help thinking of something I used to see in Italy during the Second World War. A rich industrialist would buy a factory, cost what it might, just to have wine, his meat, his bread. Money was no object. The important thing was to have something to eat. This sort of production black market was safer that the product black market. Possibly it was even more economical.

Just so, here too the government of Venezuela is more interested in extraction than in production. The only important thing about production is quantitative efficiency. The object is to have enough potatoes—or rice or yucca or bananas, or coffee—for the domestic market. The income from the sale of oil and iron abroad makes it possible for this "black market in production" to go on. It is another form of alienation. Farmers work their land—now in the hands of benevolent capitalists—not having the last drop of their blood squeezed out of them, true, but reduced to things, sterilized in the instinct by which a human being is a human being—the instinct of invention.

"They've built us nice enough houses," Ramón tells me, "but most of us can't write our names. Some of us can't use our jeeps on the roads built by the Highway Department because we can't read the road signs. We're slaves, and content with it, resigned."

I am dismayed to think that the terrible virus of misery is coming through in new strains now, with ever more serious effects, and sinking ever deeper roots in the human organism. It seems that equality for all, to which we all aspire and which costs us a daily quota of blood, recedes with the horizon. We seem to be headed toward equality in wretchedness, in the loss of our identity, in the erosion of our creativity, rather than toward authentic human growth.

True, the distance between the Bojó farmer and the Caracas agronomist does seem to be shrinking. But in the past (which progress, rather than time, has rendered remote) the equality of artisan and philosopher, of stonemason and architect, was determined by their respective capacities not for consumption but for invention, by their creative powers, their deep knowledge of the mystery of nature. From my mountain lookout I see human intimacy being materialized by a potential for consumption, and by a more or less conscious obedience to the laws of economics and physics. The religious dependency of peasants who called on the saints for rain and sun, and for the protection of their little plot of ground—an integral, necessary part of the family—has become obedience to unknown higher powers.

Misery *was* like an evil in your outer flesh. It could be healed. It was an abscess to be removed. Now it seems to reach to the inmost part of the human being. It seems to become the human being.

Again I can't help thinking of the two categories of rich at whom Christ pointed the accusing finger—the ones who didn't know what to do with what they owned, and the Pharisees. The Pharisees had been overawed by the wealth at the inmost part of their being, at the center of their personhood. There would seem to be no cure for that. Analogously, poverty seems to strike ever deeper into the human being as such, seems to penetrate to the core of our very being. It seems to me that poverty of *having* is more and more becoming a poverty of *being*.

The apocalyptic prophecies on the world's destruction have not lost their nightmarish quality in the process of their secularization.

The dark clouds that men and women saw mounting on the horizon just before the "death of God," and looking like the ones foretold to come one day to cover the earth, were, for those who knew their roots, really swelling with gladness and hope. *Our* clouds are only toxic acids, and they destroy the other kind. Dialogue is dead.

The continuation or interruption of the energy that keeps us alive used to be in the hands of one wise and loving Being; now it is in the hands of many beings, and they are neither wise nor loving. The Father might be temporarily absent from the house. But we could open all the doors and go sit in any room, because we were carrying all the keys. Now there is only the void, the abode of a nameless fear. We could go in there, but who wants to? All the doors are open, but inside, we know, there is no hope. Only fear.

The Fear of Not Being at Home in One's Own House

I know where you can find this state of the world in microcosm, Pedro. In your weary, drug-hooked neighborhood friends. The alarm has sounded, and has reached their ears. The two million abandoned children, fatherless and motherless, out of a Venezuelan population of little more than eleven million; the imbalance between metropolitan Caracas and a Caracas of outcasts, of human refuse; *campesinos* wrenching a subsistence from their *conucos*, their little plots of ground, with prehistoric tools, alongside strips reserved for intensive farming methods under government control. Then why not drugs? Why not an escape? Why live for tomorrow? Tomorrow belongs to the mighty exploiters anyway.

Pedro knows that his world isn't fit to live in, but he doesn't know why it's not fit to live in. He's noticed that his friends can't live this way, and that one way or another they all run for it. Can flight become exodus? What can I take back to my friends? Pedro's questions manifest impatience, and a certain anxiety. He lives with me out of a desire to receive a Christian initiation. Long hours of boredom in the past, long conversations that were only a rehashing of the exploits of youth, a life of listless, empty labor for subsistence wages, drugs, orgies without beauty and without a spark of love—all yielded to the intuition that Christ might point the way to something more substantial.

Alternating toil and dialogue, silence and companionship, have given him a security he never knew before. I can tell he has been freed from fear, and he has noticed the same thing. But fear of what? His motorbike accidents have not tamed his passion for speed. And he likes to go for long walks at night, to discover insights and messages that I am accustomed to look for in books. Fear of what? I don't know. Fear of not being welcome, perhaps. Fear of "What do you want to know that for? Why, you're still wet behind the ears"? Fear of "Shut off the radio, it bothers me"?

No, I think it's the fear that lurks in the little initiatives he takes with his little pieces of lumber, to build shelves, a table, cupboards, closets—so that little by little our hut is being adorned with "conveniences." Now we shall no longer have to eat sitting on the floor, do our writing on our knees, or hang our pants on a nail. And he asks me—more with a glance than in so many words—whether I approve of these initiatives of his. Yesterday I told him, when he actually asked my permission to build a stool, "Pedro, I want you to feel at home. You can do whatever you want." And he said, "That's not the way it was at home. They were always saying, 'Turn off the radio, turn off the light, don't use up all the nails.' " Ah, this is the fear, then: the eerie terror of not being at home in one's own house. Pedro has led me to see this insight by insight, by the little hints of bitterness I've caught in his allusions, as he tells me the story of his life by bits and pieces. It's the fear of the young. And it's the adult's fear.

I find no clearer way to tell the story of Christ, and the human story, than with these words of Saint John:

> To his own he came,
> yet his own did not accept him [John 1:11].

Here is the root of our hostility toward ourselves and others, the root of the drug problem, of our self-destruction, and of our other-destruction, whether morbid or violent.

"That's not the way it was at home," Pedro remonstrates. And I'm glad to have the hammer strokes around. They could be lighter. Pedro pounds on our simple furnishings so furiously that they fall to pieces. It's as if he were splitting rocks! But I'm content. I know that the strokes of his hammer are not swung in protest against my modest hut, which he is only trying to make a little more comfortable. They are only his simple, direct way of feeling secure. These tremendous, nail-bending, table-shattering blows, and Pedro continually angry with his wood that "isn't worth a damn," are the expression of a liberation that he heard himself express only yesterday, when he said, "Free. Not the way it was at home." I feel delivered from fear. The soil, the earth, is mine. I have been received, welcomed. All the tables in the world can go to pieces, pants can just keep hanging there on their nail till they get a chance to lie down comfortably.

Bravo, Pedro. Your hammer blows, the way they fall in this room, aren't vandalism, aren't destruction. They're the song of life, the joy of "touching down" at last, of room to breathe. They're your personal discovery of the gift of a "land to be taken possession of" (Deut. 9:23)—or rather a protesting, complaining rediscovery, because it comes after explusion (Gen. 3:23). Brother to the seafoam, and the crane, and the rose. . . .

Needed: Understanding More than Patience

I gather it from the gladness in his eyes. From his patience to begin over again. Actually he's not disappointed when his tables fall to pieces. He's pleased with his strength and freedom. He's discovering his creative space, and the swings of his hammer are a discovery song. He's like a person running about "every which way" to see whether this is dream or reality. Yes, it's real, all right, and it's his.

Twelve-tone music has never meant anything to me, and right now I'm in a polemic with a Mexican writer whose baroque style, all his own, leaves me nonplussed, and I think I'm standing up to him when I confess my ignorance: "I don't understand you." But this hammer music seems clear. I'm holding the key to its interpretation right here in my hand. I could let this noise get on my nerves. This life among the wood scraps could make me "blow my cool." The daily quest for my papers under stacks of what used to be tables could discourage me in my undertaking. Now I understand that dialogue between the generations calls for more than just patience. If we saw all facts as signs of history—in Pedro's case, "his story"—if we always had the key to these mysterious signs of another human being, so that we could enter into them, I think understanding would be easy.

Between me, the reader and writer, and Pedro, who smashes his tables and twists his nails without mercy and without any reflection on the limitations of matter, there is a profound oneness, and an atmosphere of acceptance rather than of patience and toleration. I don't know how to tell him that I'm singing with him, that the strokes of his hammer don't bother me in the least—although I can neither read nor write with the radio on.

Now, where shall we begin, Pedro? Where shall we start, now that you have no more tables to break or nails to bend and you're sitting quietly at last and wondering what you're to tell your friends when you get back? Where to begin? Right here, Pedro, with the strokes of your hammer—with their meaning, with the hut that's yours, and isn't, with the eviction and the homecoming, with that "To his own he came, yet his own did not accept him." It wasn't strangers, it wasn't adversaries—it was his own. Before you meet up with enemies, before there's a violent attack, there's this un-armed rebuff and rejection. "Go away, there's no room here." I've explained to Pedro that his problem is the problem Jesus had. He too was given to understand that he was a stranger among his own—that he was not welcome at home. The problem of life, the reason for our existence, centers on the problem of welcome. "Whoever welcomes a child such as this for my sake welcomes me. And whoever welcomes me welcomes, not me, but him who sent me" (Mark 9:37). This is the whole of Christian initiation: the development of this central notion that Christ and his Father are found in welcome, in acceptance, of the other.

Pedro is quite satisfied with this discovery. He doesn't much care for breaking his head on theories or sweating over books. Welcoming is easy. Children and adults walk right into our hut without knocking. We have no office hours, or any cultural barriers. But Pedro, are we sure we're really "welcoming," really accepting? Just because we have no door, are we hospitable? *The Christian is hospitable, is one who welcomes, one who receives, one who accepts, others.* After a long discussion, we correct this definition, replacing it with another, which seems to us to be more correct: The Christian is one who gradually *becomes capable of welcoming.*

Pedro feels happy and confused at the same time, because he's been led to believe that the Christian is one who "believes in God and Jesus, and goes to Mass." It has never occurred to him that being a Christian might have anything to do with acceptance. Would it be possible to put all three definitions together: going-to-Mass-and-believing-and-welcoming? Could all three be condensed into one? Let's try it. Let's start with "going to Mass."

2

A Relationship to Invent

You have Mass with bread and wine. This Pedro knows. He's seen Mass celebrated, in fact he's attended with me now and then. What is the Mass? The host and the wine, he answers.

Bread and wine, yes. The "fruit of the earth." But look, they're not fruit that grows by itself, like guava or wild blackberries. Bread and wine are fruit of the earth *and* "the work of human hands." Wine doesn't pour itself into the bottle, and bread doesn't jump into the oven and then onto the table. Just think of the chain of persons, the network of relationships, necessary to get it here, into our hands, this piece of bread and this little glass of wine! The label on the bottle says the wine is from Chile. Then this wine has traveled half the length of the Americas. And the grain probably comes from Argentina. Pedro has recently been to Guaira, the port of Caracas, and was shown a ship that was unloading Argentinian grain. These reflections place us within an extremely vast geographical and human network. Our bread and wine tell a story of distant lands, of men and women working themselves to death with scarcely the wherewithal to subsist.

Pedro was working in the garlic harvest this morning, and he wonders in whose stew his garlic is going to end up. After all, there is a bit of his toil clinging to it, and some of his song! *Y por eso tengo el alma, y por eso tengo el alma primorosa del cristal!* ("Yes, I've got a soul, yes I've got a soul that shines like crystal!") Someone sang, someone planted. There were others, commingling their labor, not with the merriment of 20-year-old Pedro, but with

10

groaning and sweating, to provide us with this bread and wine.

Yes, someone protesting in inaudible bitterness, and someone happy with the abundance of this year's harvest. And the merchants, the ones who don't get tired? Practically without seeing the product, and certainly without touching it, but just by distributing it, they receive a greater portion of the profit than those who have sweated and suffered to make the land produce. Let's calculate the difference in value between the point of departure and the point of arrival. And I tell Pedro of my recent experiences in Argentina, in Suriyaco: peaches sold under the tree, one peso for five kilos; one hundred kilometers away, two pesos a kilo.

This "fruit of the earth" speaks to us not only of the fatigue, the sweat, the song of an all but sportive toil on the part of the young, and of the servile work from which others have never been able to break free. It speaks to us as well of the exploitation practiced by those who have discovered the "trick" of getting rich quick and effortlessly.

It speaks to us of the "smart ones and the stupid ones," says Pedro. We'll have to see if this is the difference, Pedro: the "quick-witted" and the "slow-witted." For the moment, though, we'll let it be. Later we can come back to it. The conclusion we come to now is that this piece of bread and this sip of wine are filled with humanity. They throb with human life. They are not dead things. They are pieces of life.

And what does Jesus do with these pieces of life? He makes them "Communion." Communion. First Communion. Pedro's stream of consciousness ends abruptly. Yes, the Mass is the same as Communion, First Communion, for example—the "most beautiful day of your life."

But Pedro couldn't make his First Communion. His mother hadn't the money to buy him a suit. One day a young neighbor of his had left her house dressed in a long bridal gown to make her First Communion. And Pedro had asked to make his First Communion. But his father had replied that he was not to talk such nonsense (only he used a stronger word). "I've got other things to think about, things like that aren't for us. Blanquita's father is a shopkeeper; he has money to burn." And it was never mentioned again.

Well then, let's forget about "Communion" and "First Communion" with capital letters. Let's rescue the word and just talk about "communion." Communion is a word meaning to join together as friends, and more than just friends: it means becoming one with others. Pedro, it's hard to say what kind of communion Jesus has in mind. There aren't many models of that kind of love around. Maybe married love. But we'll come back to that. (How many things we're going to have to "come back to"! What were they? The thing about smart and dumb, married love, First Communion. For now let's stick with the subject of communion.)

The Eucharist, the Mass, the bread and wine, are for *having communion*, because we're divided, we're one another's enemies. Right now, while we're talking, the paper lying on the table reports the fall of Saigon—Ho Chi Minh City, now. Here's a country that's been at war practically since 1940. All those many years without peace. In another column we can read about Argentina on the brink of civil war. And these are examples of public hostility, *open* conflict. But Pedro has known division at home, unlove at home. Making noise just to bother someone, turning off the light or the radio when someone else wants it on. Father wasn't home for Mother's birthday—till he came home drunk, and the day ended in agony. It's not only in Vietnam, or with bombs and napalm and kidnappings that you can have unlove. Unlove is at home, too, even in bed. Pedro has learned that there is unlove even in sexual intercourse, which ought to be the supreme act of communion.

Communion as your father sees it—the child going to church in a long gown as if she were on her way to a ball—may be "nonsense," as your father said. But liking one another, caring for one another, and getting along—this is the only thing that gives life some flavor! "Making your First Communion" is a notion for you to get out of your head, because for you it wasn't "the most beautiful day of your life." But "making communion" is important. It's the most important thing in the world.

I think that the person who decides to drop a nuclear bomb is indirectly looking for communion. Yes, you think that's crazy, and a horrible thing to say. But such a person is trying to eliminate obstacles to *entente*, to peace, to dialogue.

"Sure," Pedro says, "*his* peace—the dialogue *he* wants."

Pedro is angry. Right, Pedro, that would be a diabolical peace, thought up by someone's twisted ego; it wouldn't be an act of love. It would be a caricature of love, and I said it only to give an extreme example of how, deep down in the human heart, even in someone perverse, this dream of peace and understanding lives. But let's leave it there. No, this isn't a point to come back to. Just consider it an intellectualistic digression. Forgive me, and let's go on.

The Earth Is Ours

Well, then, why don't we just wake up one fine morning and "have communion"? Can we just go ahead and decide to be in communion with others? If we could, we'd be stupid not to. In love there's everything to be gained. I think that if we had a world referendum and asked all human beings whether they preferred to live in peace or discord, whether they preferred to love or hate, to be loved or hated, one hundred percent would vote love. Well, except for a few crazies, of course—and maybe these crazies would be voting for hate because they'd be the ones who felt the urgency of love the most. They'd vote hate out of pain and desperation, unable to believe, in their terrible disillusionment, that it's any use talking about love. So the "no" votes, too, would have to be counted as "yeses," if we were to respect the actual wishes of all the voters! The result of the referendum would be unanimous.

But there are forces within us beyond our control, sometimes beyond our awareness. In other words, there is "conditioning" within us that prevents love. Discord, separation, then, arise against our will—from this conditioning. So: does liking one another, and getting along, and treating one another as friends, depend on us or not?

Ever since I reached the age of reason, Pedro, I've heard the poets say—when I was young the poets were socialists, dreamers— I've heard the poets, and the bishops, and all the philanthropists say: "Love one another! Offer your hand, be brothers and sisters! What have we got to gain by not liking one another?" The popes (they're bishops, too) repeat it like a refrain: With war, there's everything to lose; with peace, everything to gain. Everybody likes statements like that.

My father used to have a friend who was an atheist, and who always said atheism was "the religion of man." I didn't understand that very well, but this gentleman was a good person, and was always talking about doing good for others.

Later I came to understand that evil is very deep-rooted, and that it has to be uprooted. That root is the human desire to "be like God" (Gen. 3:5). That's what the Bible says, and the history of humankind confirms it. When we say "God," we mean the pinnacle of being. It's impossible to think of anything "beyond" or "above" God. Conclusion? Pedro, the human being aspires to the highest place. And if I want the highest place, and you want the highest place, one of the two of us has to give in, because there's only one "highest place." This desire is called pride, or conceit, and all evil comes from it. What the human being creates bears the hallmark of pride.

See, even the big, fancy cars speeding down the street, just by their shape, seem to say, "Out of the way! Let me by or I'll gobble you up! I'm tougher than you are, so the street belongs to me." Not that the driver is actually thinking that at the moment. He's probably whispering sweet nothings to the young woman sitting next to him. But the object hurtling down the street says, "I'm number one! Everybody else out of the way." And behind him there's a little car coming along, and the little car shouts out, "Okay, you've got more money and you've got more cylinders. But watch out. We'll get you some day! You know how many of you guys've ended up spread all over a brick wall? Don't swagger too much, friend!"

The objects and structures we build bear the sign of our pride, and they build up pride in each of us. Seeing them come into being, there outside ourselves, we feel satisfied, and the will to follow this path increases within us. Now, human pride surfaces in a special way in the division of the earth. You're always singing that protest song, Pedro, the kind you call a "new song,"

Yo pregunto a los presentes
Si se han puesto a pensar
Que la tierra es de nosotros
Y no del que tenga más!

I ask those present
If they have ever considered
That the land belongs to us
And not to those who have more!

The land belongs to Pedro and María, to Juan and José. Right, the land is everyone's, the earth is everyone's, and by this I don't mean just the topsoil down there stretching in furrows as far as you can see, all the way to the Andes. I mean oil, copper, gold; I mean all the materials needed for tools and everything else needed to live, what we sleep on, what we enjoy ourselves with. It's all ours.

But the person who "wants to be like God" runs ahead of all the rest of us and fences in the countryside with barbed wire and says, "This is mine here. No trespassing." And he's grabbed what belongs to everybody. But he can't work the soil by himself, or pump oil or mine ore by himself, and can't do manufacturing by himself, and so he says to those outside the barbed wire: "Will you give me a hand? Will you work with me? I'll lay down the conditions, of course. If you accept them, fine; if you don't, get lost. You'll find out that everybody with barbed wire around here will tell you the same thing, so you'll be back. You won't want to starve to death. And you'll always have work."

The upshot is that the goods of the earth, which should have served to unite us, to foster cooperation, are the occasion of discord and division. Workers passing through the gate in the barbed wire realize that this is the way things will be all their life, but those who got there first will build themselves houses, go on vacations, have plenty of entertainment, send their children to private schools, and prepare to become heirs of a great estate.

In this way the goods of the earth make no one happy. They bring contentment to no one. Those who have strung the barbed wire have to find a way to defend "their" space, whereas the ones on the outside plot how to cut the barbed wire and invade the forbidden space. All these gifts of God completely fail to make us happy. We're like a bunch of drunks. Wine is supposed to cheer us up. Instead it makes us drunk. We're like our friend Manuel, who moans and groans on Mondays or Tuesdays, whichever day he sobers up, and says, "Damn that booze! I must be crazy to keep on drinking. Just look at what it does to me!" But come Saturday he's off again, and Monday morning he's cursing something that ought to be a source of cheer.

We read in chapter eight of the Letter to the Romans:

> Creation was made subject to futility not of its own accord but by him who once subjected it. . . . Yes, we know that all creation groans and is in agony even until now [8:20, 22].

We could be happy in the world, and instead we're fed up with it.

Remember, Pedro, how we talked about a film—a film both beautiful and horrible—artistically beautiful and horrible in what it said? It was called *La grande abbuffata*, "the good old slop bucket." It was about the two most direct ways of "possessing the land"—of entering into paradise while still right here on earth. It was about food and sex, and it showed how trying to use either food or sex to have paradise right here on earth makes you throw up, makes you vomit, either literally or figuratively. The bourgeois world is hell-bent for self-destruction. *This* way of going after the infinite can lead only to the destruction of the person, death. Two things are perfectly clear: that discord and division among persons is not voluntary, and that there is a "third party" in this exchange of hostilities—nature, the goods of the earth, and their distribution. By "goods of the earth" I mean oil, copper, iron, gold, corn, wheat, and so on.

What do I mean when I say that hostility is involuntary?

If I want to enter into an agreement with someone, I know how to do it. I know what I have to do. Per se, Pedro, nobody wants to fight. But in practice we make certain choices that instead of contributing to peace, to "encounter" in the good sense of the word, lead to encounter in the bad sense—to hostile confrontation, to discord. And there's no third alternative. Either we contribute to peace or we contribute to war. If we could see all persons "the way they really are," we would see that most of those who preach peace, and are convinced that they are sowing love, are actually sowing hate. How many missionaries, priests, nuns, and "militant Catholics" are just peace propagandists, with useless words that increase discord in the world and have nothing to do with the distribution of goods or the use of money to influence human history directly! They're in the service of God but they don't serve God; they're not in the service of the devil but they serve the devil.

The Empty Heart Cannot Be Filled with "Things"

So, you see, Pedro, Jesus has set the table with bread and wine. He could have set it with copper, oil, iron, gold, and so on. But look, he can't pile everything in the world on a table. He had to choose something, from among all the different things we have.

And he had to choose what would enable persons to "communicate" as deeply as possible.

Now, what type of relationship could we have with *things*? For instance, with this piece of wood. Not much. I can touch it, I can work it, break it, throw it. But there's something deeper than this that I can do with things: I can eat them. I can make them disappear inside me. I can "assimilate" them. This is the supreme "communion." Further than this, we cannot go. Stones would have to turn into bread before we could eat them. Here's what Jesus gave: communication with things, he says to us, divides you, poisons your friendship and love. You take these goods and you wage war with them, you have strikes, you burn factories, you kidnap persons, you kill, you beat your wives and children. Now, I'm taking these goods and making them my body and my blood, to make them a means of communion among you. You see, Pedro, communion with God, friendship with God, happens in a kind of triangle: communion with my sisters and brothers, communion with things, communion with Christ.

Pedro, there's so much I've just recently caught on to! It's as if all the things I'd studied for so many years took flesh here in this mud hut, with you, with the people of the soil. It's as if it were all illuminated in one flash. I hadn't understood the Eucharist, "communion," as I do now. You see, Pedro, the Eucharist, the Mass, communion, the host—they're all the same thing. The Mass, which is something so complicated that most persons can't understand it, is basically simple. They carry up to the altar, which is a table, like this one, the goods they use. They're repentant, they're practically weeping, and they say, "Look, God, my Father, I've misused these things, these goods. And see, Father, here's what I get out of it: war, division, my son's on drugs, my daughter's an alcoholic and sells her body. And especially this unbearable loneliness, this coldness in my heart!" Don't think the rich are happy, Pedro. When persons feel unloved, they can have the world right in their hands and they have nothing. There is nothing that will fill the heart's void.

For years I couldn't understand why there was such insistence on repentance in the Mass, all the insistence on forgiveness. I thought we were bothering God too much, as we kept saying, "Have mercy on me! I'm a big sinner. I'm not worthy. Mercifully allow me to approach your table." But now I see what we're capable of concocting. I just think of all I've heard about the tortures in Argentina and Uruguay, and I see we're capable of concocting horrible things. Wild beasts are little lambs by comparison. Repentance makes sense to me now.

Oh, you're right, all this asking for forgiveness at Mass is a joke. We're not repentant at all, and we go and tell God what sinners we are. What are we repentant about, anyway? I remember how one day in Caracas I ran into a demonstration. I asked one of the demonstrators what it was all about. He looked at me a little funny, so I asked another one, and he said, "I don't know exactly, but I saw all this crowd and I thought I'd go along."

I'd like to ask the person next to me at Mass, "What are you repenting of?" I might get an answer, but I'm sure it wouldn't have anything to do with anything. I repent of having offended our Father, sowing division among my brothers and sisters by my evil use of goods, making abominable use of the goods God has given me. A Marxist would say, ". . . of having divided my sisters and brothers by my inability to love, because an unjust society has made me unable to love." For a Christian, first comes the evil in a human being, through that person's pride, and then this evil manifests itself in the unjust distribution of goods.

The fact is, and we all ought to recognize it: I have not loved my sisters and brothers, in that I use goods, things, evilly. What have goods to do with it? We were talking about the bread and wine we offer with the priest. But this isn't a platonic encounter, a meeting over dead bread and wine. This bread and wine are loaded with our sins, our unlove. They should be too hot to handle. It should be the way it was with Zacchaeus. We find him in the nineteenth chapter of Saint Luke. Let's read it together.

You see, Pedro, when Jesus walks into Zacchaeus's house, everything Zacchaeus has starts to burn his fingers. What is he to do with these goods? Before getting to know Jesus, he's proudly shown his friends his house, its furnishings, his granaries, his stables, his fields. But the moment Jesus steps inside, Zacchaeus admits that these goods are not his. He has stolen them.

"But I don't think this is what happens at Mass," Pedro breaks in. "The few times I've been there, I didn't get the impression that anybody was discovering they'd stolen anything from anybody."

Touché. We don't really think about being repentant "with the bread and wine in our hands," before God and our brothers and sisters. We should be standing there saying, "I have sinned. I have made myself superior. I have been playing God. I have used things, here represented in this bread and wine in my hands, badly. Through my misuse of things, there are babies crying, women selling their bodies, drug addicts, nuclear arms, torture, war, and the blood of my sisters and brothers soaking the earth. My father and my sisters and brothers, I beg forgiveness, and I should like to know what I should do in order not to keep on living the way that I have been up to now."

Bread and Wine: Symbols and Means of Reconciliation

Going to Mass is a difficult step to take. It's hard. The first sinner is the priest, who takes advantage of the Mass to squeeze money out of his neighbor. Asking for money at Mass is supposed to be a symbol of the repentance we were talking about. It's supposed to be like Zacchaeus's decision to start doing justice with his money. But as you say, Pedro, it's a farce. This bread and this wine are laden with our crimes. There is something here besides an immaculate host.

This is what an act of true repentance should be: I beg your forgiveness, my God, for having offended my sisters and brothers, and tortured them, and put them to death, with money, for the sake of money, out of love for money. And I've offended them with words, treating them with pride in my heart. And by omission, pretending not to see others suffering, having eyes only for the "beautiful people," the ones with the shining, satisfied faces. I've offended them with deeds, looking out for myself, seeking my own prestige, so that others would say I'm the smartest business person, the attorney who's never lost a case, the physician consulted by the upper class. To oppress my neighbor I've used iron, copper, gold, coffee, wheat, and cacao. And here they are, all these things, represented in this bread and wine. I don't want to keep on filling the world with hatred, division, blood, and death. I want to promote love, concord, and life, if only a little. I want to change, and I ask you what to do. What to do, what to do? I don't want to sound like a broken record—*mea culpa, mea culpa, mea maxima culpa.* But what am I to do?

Well, reconciliation among human beings occurs *in the bread and wine*—that is, in the same *material*, first laden with crime, and then transformed into the body and blood of Christ, which becomes communion among us. First, in our hands, they are the symbol of discord. Then, after the "This is my Body, this is my Blood," they are the symbol of concord, the means, the way of reconciling with one another. Communion is created by means of the "goods of the earth."

Imagine two women seated next to one another at Mass. One comes from the east side of Caracas, the other lives in a tin shack in the section called Petare. The moment comes for the sign of peace. They embrace. Is that embrace sincere? On the "affective" level— on the psychological, "spiritual" level—it may be sincere. But it's not *eucharistic*. It's not what Mass is about. What do I mean, it's not eucharistic? I mean that an acknowledgment of fellowship and reconciliation can't come about by good intentions only. The woman from the east side can't say to the woman from Petare: "Forgive me, my sister, for having offended you." They don't even know each other. Oh, the intention is there, the sentiments are there—because the woman from the east side has no resentment against her "sister" from Petare. She feels perfectly at ease alongside a poor person.

But the whole truth would be expressed in these words: "I've offended you in what I have done and what I have failed to do, because I've thought only of myself, I've spared no expense for my convenience and luxury. It has never crossed my mind that you live under a cardboard roof, and that you can cook only beans, and only once a day, if that often. My father and my husband have exploited you, by having the house we have, by their foreign investments, our cars, and so forth. With these words you hear, this face of mine you see, these sentiments I show you, I love you. But with my deeds—which you don't see—I hate you, and little by little I shall destroy you, for I am straitening your being."

There's no reconciliation where there's been no offense. If I were to stop someone on the street and say, "Forgive me, sir, if I have offended you"—he would take me for an insane person. So we go to church to tell our neighbors we've done them wrong. But we must be specific, and say what we have done that is wrong. Otherwise we are either mad or sick. Christ places in our hands this bread and wine, this fruit of the earth, that we may recognize that "through these, with these, and in these" we have done wrong. You, woman from the east side, have wronged the woman from Petare through bread and wine, and only through bread and wine can you be reconciled.

You see, Pedro, for so many years I had not understood why there was so much insistence on sin at the Eucharist. I had not understood the significance of the Eucharist. In our theology manuals it says that no one can be saved without the Eucharist— that the Eucharist is necessary, absolutely necessary, for the salvation of the human being. It is even more necessary than the church. You can read that right in the gospel, in the sixth chapter of Saint John: "If you do not eat the flesh of the Son of Man and drink his blood, you have no life in you" (v. 53). And this means everybody, Christians and non-Christians, those who make their First Communion and those who don't because they don't have the appropriate attire.

But those who go to communion are a tiny group—very tiny in comparison with the whole of humanity. And even in this little group, how many will there be who go to communion "efficaciously"? Well, that's not the right word. Let's say "effectively," "eucharistically." What about everybody else? Is the great mass of humanity, who will never receive this body and this blood, lost forever? This is a question that long tormented me.

When I uncovered Jesus' intention—what he meant by "eating the flesh of the son of Man and drinking his blood"—I came to realize that many persons "go to communion" without knowing it. After all this talk, Pedro, it seems clear to me that "going to communion" means progressing in love and friendship *by means of the earth*, going by way of the goods of the earth. It means advancing in love, not as a feeling but as an activity—in practice, through our concrete choices. We could all close our eyes and tell ourselves: "I like everybody—no exceptions." But no, *eucharistic love* moves through *matter*, by way of a redistribution of goods. Any "love" that stands "above" this, or passes this by, is platonic love, or erotic love, or call it anything you want, but it isn't eucharistic love.

Jesus utters a hard saying, and to all human beings, not just to the little group in front of him, when he says that unless your love passes by way of bread and wine, by the flesh and blood of the Son of Man, your love will not be "vital," you will not "have life in you." Many will tell you, "You can't go to church any more without hearing a sermon on economics. You hear plenty about politics and economics, but you don't hear much about religion." But look, Pedro, eating the flesh and blood of Jesus means diving into the problem of the distribution of goods, and the use of goods, because it's in this distribution and this use that we become one another's friend or enemy, that we are brothers and sisters or oppressors.

If the human mystery weren't such a mystery, Pedro, if so many things weren't shrouded in a veil of invisibility, we'd see some funny sights. They might hurt a little, but they'd be fun, too, like watching a movie. Sometimes we'd see a revolutionary—you know, like the fellow that walked into town the other day and everybody looked at him as though he were the devil incarnate?—we'd see a revolutionary and we'd see that he or she is more eucharistic than a cloistered Blessed Sacrament religious. After all, revolutionaries fight and give their lives to make the world more just, to help human beings enter more deeply into fellowship, to bring it about that we can all have a life without the anguish of poverty and misery. It's true that cloistered monks and nuns contribute to peace, to human encounter, with their intercession. But suppose some of them are unjust, because they live in wealth, and are involved in oppression—what good does it do them to adore the Blessed Sacrament? You see, Pedro. . . .

Oh? "Intercession"? Right, that's a difficult concept. That makes another thing we'll have to come back to later. We're certainly getting a pile of things to talk about! We could talk all night, lying here on our cots, talk till the morning light. But there's work the next day, and we have to set some limits.

I knew ladies in Rome, who had nothing, or almost nothing, to do, who belonged to an Association of Adorers of the Blessed Sacrament. They spent hours sitting or kneeling before the Sacred Host. What did they say to Jesus? I don't rightly know. But I know one thing, that the only thing to say to Jesus is to *be* Jesus—that is, to save the world. But saving the world means becoming sisters and brothers. And becoming sisters and brothers means not being willing to accept the present distribution of the goods of the earth, and changing it. If we are not brothers and sisters, because the goods of the earth are distributed badly, becoming brothers and sisters must mean changing the relationships among human beings, changing their relationships toward these goods. Very likely those ladies asked Jesus to keep the world as it was—"in peace." Or at most that he would change human hearts—the bank robbers, the pilfering maids, their husbands' workers on strike. Jesus, make bad people good, and leave everything else as it is. "My daughter, the reason for my existence is to change the world," Jesus would have to answer.

In other words, Pedro, not everybody who goes to Mass is a eucharistic person, and some persons who don't go to Mass *are* eucharistic persons. That's the funny thing. So are these Roman ladies wasting their time, "gaining nothing"? I really couldn't say, Pedro. Relations between human beings and God are mysterious— we don't know anything about them, and we have no right to judge. But one thing is sure: if you pray, but don't change your behavior toward your brothers and sisters one bit, well, then you're certainly wasting your time.

Eucharist: Singing Thanks to Life

Remember, Pedro, how you asked me what that fancy word "Eurcharist" meant? You're right, of course, about religious words being difficult, like medical words—hepatitis, gastroenteritis, dysentery. Well, here's what Eucharist means. When you wake up in the morning feeling good, and you sing while you put your clothes on, and after breakfast you half-walk half-slide down the hillside singing—it's like that.

And I hear you in the evening, when you're still a long way off, singing Violetta Parra's song:

Gracias a la vida,
Que me ha dado tanto—
Me ha dado la risa,
Y me ha dado el llanto.

Thanks be to life,
Which has given me so much—
Has given me laughter,
And has given me tears.

When I hear you singing that song, I can tell things are fine. No catastrophes. What do you feel on the inside? I don't know. I know you're glad to be alive, though. I've seen persons in the most elegant bathrobes and dressing gowns, getting up late in the morning and coming out onto their balconies and looking out at the street as if they were so tired of life they wanted to vomit. "Oh no, another day!" they seemed to say.

Eucharist means singing thanks to life. I'm glad to be alive. Now let's take this and put it together with what we've been talking about. When do you feel grateful to life? When you feel in communion with your brothers and sisters, when you feel accepted by them. When we live in quest of communion, with the sole motivation of building communion, we feel grateful to life, glad to be alive. To feel right with the world, to be able to sing thanks to life and sing it sincerely, there's no other way than to live for others, with our only aim being to build communion among human beings. And we get this only with a change in relationships. This is the way of the Eucharist.

Your mother tells you your brother Fernando will always be happy because he doesn't worry about anyone else, he looks out for himself, he lives for himself. She says you'll always be hurt, Pedro, whereas your brother Fernando will be a happy person. That's false, Pedro. Selfish persons look as if they are having a good time, but it's a good time the way an animal has a good time in a lush pasture. When the voice of conscience awakens, selfish persons will look at themselves and see the catastrophe.

Jesus laid down an absolute law: To gain your life, you have to lose it (Mark 8:35). The more you bind yourselves to human beings, the happier you will be. The joy of living will become more solid and secure because it will be rooted in something permanent. I hope this song goes with you always, Pedro, even in your moments of anguish. Yes, thanks to life, because life is good for something.

3

The Long Road to Communion

If there are persons who seek communion among human beings without receiving the Eucharist, then what need is there of the Eucharist? That's a big question, Pedro. To answer that question we have to lay our whole faith on the line. If we think human beings can break free of selfishness, of noncommunication, all by themselves—then indeed what need is there of Christ? But if we think that without Christ human beings are helpless, then we discover that all human powers rest on the active liberative power that comes from the Lord Jesus. The Son of God has come to live with us and share our lives, to shatter our isolation, to make the world the setting for the reign of God, which is the reign of fellowship and friendship.

You see, Pedro, the history of humanity is the history of its revolutions, and all revolutions worthy of the name are episodes in the Christian revolution. All humans are hunting for the same thing, but they are hunting along different trails, seeing whether they can come to an understanding, achieve more fellowship with one another. And this need for "more communion" begets the need for justice, the need to distribute the goods of the earth in such a way as to make the "established disorder" disappear, the structures in which some have too much and others too little. Individuals work for Christ's program even when they don't know it. Few believe in or celebrate the Eucharist. But the Eucharist reaches out to all.

Jesus mentioned leaven and salt. These are small things, you can't even see them in all the dough, but they affect the whole loaf. Here in this house, which is ours now, Jesus is present not just for us, but for everyone. The Eucharist says to all: Fear not, it is I. Don't worry, I'm here. Fight for liberation, for a communion of brothers and sisters, for fellowship among yourselves. You'll win. You can't tell when or how, but have hope—the struggle will not be in vain. It's not the individualistic, selfish, lonely side that will win. The communion side will win.

Shall we go back and look for an answer to the question of what to do? Suppose a man has a change of heart in church, during the liturgy, and realizes that he has had in his hands "goods of the earth" that he has used to create injustice, separation, and non-communication. He begs forgiveness of God, and of his neighbors on either side. He tells them, in one way or another, "Look, my friend, I care about you, but by acting the way I have, I've cheated you. Forgive me." Now, if it were all to end there, the caricature we have of the Mass would never change. So what is to be done? The simplest thing would be to go home, sell all, and give the proceeds to the poor. Perhaps not in every case, but sometimes this could and should be done. The gospel never gives mechanical solutions, never gives "prefabricated" answers.

Three Things to Do

I should say that there are three things to do—not as a blueprint, but as guidelines, as an orientation. First of all, one ought to form a clear notion that life has not been bestowed on us in order to make money, or be well off. Our raison d'être, as the French say, our reason for being, is to become brothers and sisters. Did you hear them singing in our parish, one evening when we went there to-gether, that song of hope for a "new day, when we would all be brothers and sisters again"?

Ah, yes, Pedro, you're sharp, all right. "What do you mean, 'again'?" you ask. We shall *begin* to be brothers and sisters, we should say, because we weren't any better in the past than we are now. We weren't sisters and brothers "once upon a time," and somehow had a falling out. *History is a long march toward a communion of brothers and sisters.* The hope is that one day we'll begin to behave like brothers and sisters. I don't believe that this day will ever come in its fullness. But we should always move closer to it as an ideal.

Many say that this value cannot be created in a capitalistic society. To give life this direction would be simply to contradict capitalism. Capitalistic society inculcates a conceptualization of the human being as one who seeks to dominate others, who struggles to have more possessions. This is its "anthropo-logy," its view of human nature. But must the Christian not be the "antagonistic contradiction," as they say, of all denial of justice, all negation of fellowship and communion, all that is unhuman?

Unfortunately, Christians have not been brought up to fight. They've been brought up to accept their lot, to conform. But this is contrary to the gospel. Our reason for being cannot be other than a search for fellowship and communion. And so we must live in poverty. We must not let ourselves be caught in the net of advertising propaganda, which creates a horde of desires and smothers the one great Christian desire: that all men and women be *one*.

The second thing to do is not to refuse political tasks that bear directly on eliminating injustice in the world and helping human beings to become sisters and brothers. It's a difficult undertaking, because there is no political party whose platform is a clear and consistent search for fellowship and communion. But when someone comes along who is genuinely disinterested, and in all sincerity seeks truly to contribute a little, even a little, to fellowship and communion in the world, and lives with this preoccupation, that person will find a way to "get involved." Some of the young people of your country are finding a way, Pedro, and you've met some of them. We know, right from the start, that the forward step we take will be a very little one, that our commitment is wrapped in darkness and obscurity. But what counts is love. What counts is the real desire to struggle for communion.

When some say they'd "like to get involved" but "don't know where or how," and "politics is so mixed up you can't tell which side to be on," you can be sure they're afraid, or else that they're watching out for their own interests, at least subconsciously. If we decide to publish this message, Pedro, I intend to come back to this point, not for your sake—you've got it—but for the sake of those we'll invite to dialogue with us. Those who die for freedom and communion in the world every day haven't done a lot of theorizing about it, or quibbled over just where their own interests lie. Teachers, parents—all educators—will have to inculcate this idea in their children. What does it mean to be a person and to be a Christian? Why are we alive? To build communion. Not to *say* we have communion with one another. This is just a subterfuge. But to *have* communion.

The third thing to do is to "be compassionate" (Luke 6:36). Well, actually, it's not something to "do," because we don't get to be compassionate just by making up our minds to be so. Being compassionate is a result of something. You see, Pedro, anyone associating with Christ would have had to see the special concern he had for the lowly, the outcasts, the ones last in line—anyone who was worthless in the eyes of society. Christ loved these persons particularly. And this particularity will always distinguish the Christian from those who devote themselves to political activism, because the lowly and outcast do not represent a political force. The "compassionate heart"—particular sensitivity toward sisters and brothers who have been left behind, been left out—is the gift of Christ to his friends, and is the most characteristic sign that someone is Christ's friend.

Now you realize, Pedro, that the communion bread is much more important in the history of humankind than is commonly thought. So, maybe we should drop First Communion with its big to-do, and all its ceremonies, that give us a wrong idea of communion. Maybe we should. First Communion should be celebrated only by the child of a family of activists who are rearing him or her for the struggle, for openness to others—for real Christianity, for the following of Jesus. And there would be no place for fancy suits or dresses, or for any of the ambiance that makes the Eucharist an object of consumerism, received without knowing exactly what it's for. You buy something, you carry it home, because advertising has convinced you or cast a spell on you, even though the thing itself is of no use at all. A consumer society has emptied the Eucharist of all meaning, and it should not be received by someone who does not know its meaning.

What Freedom?

One of the remarks you made, Pedro—one of the things we said we'd come back to—was a question. Why does society label "stupid" those who give their lives for an ideal, the unselfish ones—and "prudent" or "smart" the selfish ones? Society is the cultural product of an ensemble of persons, and is based on certain principles that might be called its philosophy. These principles are formed in the heads of certain persons who both invent them and interpret them. That is, they understand how far we've come, and they indicate the direction to take from here. Society creates certain values, and these values guide the life of the members of the society. The society we are living in at present is called "liberal," or "capitalistic," whereas the one we aspire to is a "socialist" society. These definitions are too simple—they don't say everything—but they're important for making clear what I mean.

If I said, this man is a miser, or that one is a spendthrift, I wouldn't be saying everything about him. I wouldn't be saying whether he's gone to college, whether he's very intelligent or not, whether he's an affectionate person, but I'd have given you an important key to the understanding of a great deal about his behavior—why his wife doesn't get along with him, why his children are troublemakers. Much of his behavior would find its explanation in this definition: he's a miser or a spendthrift.

Now, a "liberal" society means a society based on liberty, on freedom, as an essential characteristic. And this is a fine notion: we are free beings, and we ought to have liberty. But liberty applied indiscriminately can have a negative effect—for example, in the use of goods. I may do what I want to with my goods, yes, on condition that I not interfere with the rights of my neighbor, who is my equal.

Here's an example. In Venezuela, if I set up a distillery, say, a rum distillery, I can make a lot of money. I'll make 180 bolivars a year on 100. If I plant potatoes or rice, I risk losing everything, or, in a good year, I could make 110 bolivars on 100. If I can, obviously I'm going to have a distillery. My money is mine, and I can do with it what I want to. This is the negative aspect of liberty. The money's mine and I can do anything I want with it.

Now, just multiply this example by a few thousand, and you've got capitalism. In a society where it's possible to make money grow without obstacles, the idea becomes prevalent that the most important thing is to make money grow, and the intelligent person is the one who knows how to make money grow. It's your money, and it doesn't seem to you that you've robbed anybody. You haven't robbed any banks or burgled any businesses. But think a moment about the rum distillery. Think of all the disasters you're causing. Your money doesn't go into normal agriculture, so now some persons will go hungry, others will become drunkards, and so the number of persons useless or harmful to society will increase; now you've got persons out on the sidewalks, and so forth. The ideal of liberty as the supreme and absolute good of the human being leads in the long run to slavery and oppression.

The North Americans, the "gringos," as you call them, are fanatics for liberty. They cry bloody murder because there's a new censorship law in Peru. They have no use for Latin American dictatorships. They want democratic institutions, parliaments, congresses. In actuality, with an economic system thought out and very cunningly controlled, and defended by the armed forces, CIA espionage, and means we don't even know, they dominate Latin America. Pick up today's newspaper, and you read: "Washington Unhappy with Organization of American States Meeting." Peru's foreign minister enters into an agreement with his colleagues on his own initiative, and a roar of protest goes up from the United States government. The mice want to come to an agreement and set up defensive tactics, so that the cat won't gobble them up. And the cat doesn't *like* that. The cat snarls.

The socialist system, to put it very simply, has as its basic idea, as the guiding principle of its society, not the *growth* of wealth, but the *distribution* of wealth, using a more just distribution of wealth to make citizens more free, more creative, more human as persons. The idea is to get economic power into more hands, so that there won't be potentates and puppets, but all will be enabled to be more human as persons. In order to arrive at this goal, you have to say "Stop!" to those who, until now, have encountered no obstacles to the proliferation of their wealth. And only the poor can say "Stop!" It is up to the poor to demand their own rights.

Conclusion: in a society aspiring to the growth of wealth as the supreme good, the hero—the successful person—is the one who manages to amass the greatest amount of money in the shortest time. The one who fails to do so is the loser. In a socialist society, the successful person is the one who is the best neighbor. Ramón is an example, right before our eyes. Ramón isn't just concerned about his own family. First thing in the morning he goes around rousing his neighbors so they won't miss the bus for an important meeting.

I could go on forever about the different ways he's shown his commitment to the advancement of his community here in Bojó. He could have been a "demagogue" instead—concerned with his own ambition. You have to watch persons like that over some period of time. If they use others for their own political career, for their own aggrandizement, they're demagogues. If they genuinely see themselves as the servants of others, then they're unselfish.

Socialism is impossible in a consumer society. There are no models of service, of generosity, to follow. The model that attracts followers is that of the "grabber," someone who thinks only of his or her own welfare. I could see this in Chile in Allende's time. Chile was trying to be a socialist society in a consumer hemisphere. For one reason or another, the doors were not shut on consumerism. The common person, the laborer, was asked to make sacrifices for society, to strive for a new society, a new image of what it means to be human. But advertising propaganda was allowed to operate. Socialist education did its work, but the framework of the capitalist world was left intact. Chile tried to build a socialist society with a citizenry vitiated by capitalism, and it can't be done.

4

Liberation from Fear and Dependence

Pedro, I keep saying that I can feel your deliverance from fear. You don't say much about it. You know I understand. And you wouldn't talk about it in public, to strangers. You wouldn't want to compromise your "Venezuelan macho pride." You're not a timorous one. Your liberation from fear shows, in your new self-confidence, your confidence in life, your hopes for tomorrow.

Where does this fear come from? It is born the moment we leave our mother's womb and enter the world. It's as if we were leaving a cave—dark, but small and cozy, and you can touch the walls and know you're not alone. You feel the hot breathing, you're surrounded by the rhythmic pulse of life. It's not only a cave, it's a thermal blanket. Oh, it hasn't always been that great inside. You've been knocked about a bit, the smooth flow of your first existence has seen its interruptions, little accidents. But you were not alone. Then suddenly you're thrust out of your close quarters into an immense, boundless night. And your desperate struggle begins; you call for help, you look for support, you try not to be alone. This is where it all starts, the story of human beings in quest of communion. Here we have a tragic, but stupendous, definition of history.

The father comes into the picture, too. In old Roman law, when a baby was born the father was to lift the child in his arms in acknowledgment that he was the father. I've seen something like this in Sardinia, which is perhaps the most "Roman" place left in Italy. In Sardinia it's always the father who carries the baby to baptism. Is this a vestige of the ancient Roman custom? The father comes on the scene as the star of the drama the moment a baby is born. He needn't cradle the baby in his arms and change its clothes. He may, but he needn't. But he communicates security, protection, to both the child and its mother. Here I am, don't be afraid. It may be at this moment that the fate of this person, still only a baby, is decided: whether the story of this little one will be a story of quest for communion, or of violence against the human race.

In the Venezuelan family, it often happens that the mother and child are two forsaken ones, bereft of any sense of security. It would be hard to say which of the two has the greater fear of the void, of tomorrow, which of the two feels more alone and defenseless in the face of life, even if the mother is a person of great physical courage, and completely prepared to fight for enough food for her baby. It's not a matter of physical courage. It's a matter of the sense of security that I receive from someone who loves me, someone who accepts this life we have in common, and shares with me responsibility for this little child. In new life you touch the mystery and drama of time. The mystery of time is not so frightening if you feel loved, if you feel a hand on your shoulder: here I am.

Most think that it's the mother the baby really needs. The father comes later, in adolescence, when the developing child will need a teacher and disciplinarian. In actuality, the baby has more need of a father than of a mother. With its mother's milk, the baby must also imbibe security, the certitude of being welcome, confidence. And so this milk must be "full of the father." When a mother nurses her baby, she should feel the hand of love on her shoulder.

When you don't feel loved today, right now, you regard tomorrow, the future, with fear. Love, and only love, saves a person from the fear of time, because one who feels loved is incapable of imagining empty spaces.

But then, Pedro interrupts, my friends and I are all going to have nothing but fear and insecurity, because none of us has had a father like that.

Let's don't jump to conclusions, Pedro. Let's go on a bit with our subject. Fatherhood isn't something wafting in the air all by itself. No one is a father and nothing else. If a man is a husband—"one flesh" with his wife—then spontaneously, without forcing anything, without having to do anything special, he will be a father as well. If he isn't a father in his first encounter with his baby, he will probably never be one later.

There are three ways a man can misuse his fatherhood. He may simply be unconcerned about his child, who is not much more to him than a piece of furniture. Or he may be brutally concerned, and unload his aggressivity on the child, his discontent, his strength and power that have been stymied within him, or lacerated by the humiliations he receives in society and the frustrations life has had in store for him. Or, thirdly, there is the kind of father we might call "capitalistic," who projects his own typology onto his child. The child must grow up to be one of those who "make it," just as his horse must never lose, and his business must always be the most profitable. How often, in this milieu, have I heard it said, "I want the best for my children"—where "the best" means that they must be "number one," they must make it to the top of the heap. The child is an object. Oh, of course there is love there, some love, as between a person and an object or an expensive pet. But it is not a personalized love.

Now, in all three cases, the father inspires more fear than love in his child, either because the father is a stranger and has come into the house like a thief in the night, or because he is an armed enemy seeking to destroy his own child, or because he is the boss and his offspring is the indentured servant bound to produce the absolute maximum. This kind of father must be got rid of.

Freud, that high-flying, heady intellectual, saw in this struggle between the threatening father and the child who must defend himself or herself against threats, an erotic rivalry. To put his theory very simply: I love my mother, but my father got to her before me. He is my rival, and I must get rid of him. This rivalry may be there, surely. But it is not the only reason for a violent, destructive relationship between father and child. This fear explains all the future behavior of the adult. It explains the "big macho," who has to dominate women in his pride, taking them as objects, it explains all forms of aggressivity and violence. It explains timidity toward others. It explains cowardliness in life's concrete choices. It explains sloth. What's the point of taking my work seriously? There's nothing in it for me. And especially it explains the incapacity to love. The inability to love is an incapacity really to give oneself to another. The oppressive, overprotective mother, who smothers you, has her roots here. The oppressed woman incarnates the image of the oppressor. You'd think it would be just the opposite. Knowing how hard a life of servitude is, you'd think you should be all the more in love with freedom. Instead, the dominated woman becomes a dominator. A macho society is matriarchal, and vice versa.

Conversion: A Journey

No, don't despair, Pedro. Remember, liberation is rooted in slavery. We haven't made this quick diagnosis of things just to arrive at a negative conclusion: poor us, we're done for! No, here's the conclusion we want to come to: we all have need of liberation. Liberation from what? From fear and dependence. Out of experience, and not from any philosophical principles, I have to tell you, Pedro, that not everyone who comes from a "good family" turns out to be a free person. Often they are selfish, mediocre, bourgeois, gluttonous. No, don't laugh! It's not true that if this is the way things are, it's better to leave the world as it is. Each of us, no matter where we're starting from, is offered a chance at complete liberation. The "rich young man" in the gospel certainly came from a "good family," if he had been taught to observe the commandments ever since he was a child. But he didn't turn out very well.

What route does Jesus choose to fill this void that is left by the absence of a father? The opposite route from the way nature works. By nature, first comes the father, and he projects himself onto his children. In the liberation movement, it's the children who approach the father. Let's try to dig into this a little. Basically, there's only one kind of conversion: the conversion of a human being from being selfish to being unselfish. All human beings, before their conversion, are closed in upon themselves. They see others only in terms of themselves, as means to an end. To use a word that won't really be too hard for you to understand, Pedro, they are all "centripetal." This means that everything must orbit around their own ego. Through conversion, they become "centrifugal." That is, they see themselves in terms of others now. Conversion is not something that happens once and for all. Conversion is a journey. You can tell when persons are on the road to conversion by their love for others, a love that urges them to give of themselves to others.

You see, Pedro, when persons say they're "converted" because they've started to go to church, but they're still selfish, you can be sure their conversion is not yet complete. The sign of conversion is *unselfishness.* I know a Latin American who is a practicing Catholic to the point of bigotry. He asked me to find a group of sisters to run a home for the elderly that he would finance. Then I found out that this fellow was rich, and was getting richer all the time, because he ran a lottery and other gambling operations. With his right hand he robbed and exploited others ten times as much as he gave them something back with his left hand, for peace of conscience and in order to be considered a good person. The Christian world is full of examples like this. A certain shallowness in our definition of what it means to love our neighbor makes it possible for Christians to "bilk their neighbor."

The ones to trust are the ones who give not just their money, but their person, those who give their lives for their neighbor—the poor priest, who lives every day and every hour of the day in the service of his brothers and sisters; the young person who goes to live among the poor at the expense of a "career." There are plenty of examples of those who love not with money, but with their lives, with their own persons. Jesus has not given us money, things, helps, and props—he has given us ourselves. He talks about laying down his life in the service of others (John 10:14–18). Pedro, my wish for you is that you should be able to taste these verses from the gospel with the same relish with which you are enjoying that cup of guava juice this very moment. You don't know Latin, but it's transparent Latin for someone who knows Spanish: *pono animam meam.* I lay down, I put down, my soul, I place my life in the service of others. To me, the image is one of someone "going for broke," someone betting every last peso.

Those who love put their lives on the line. For them conversion consists in a kind of feverish unselfishness, a growing desire to give one's life for one's sisters and brothers. Other conversions are "notional" conversions, conversion in the head only. When your whole life is genuine commitment to others, you discover what communion is. It isn't those who bleat in church, "Brothers and sisters, we're all brothers and sisters, Oooo!," who can tell you what communion means. It's those who build it, who build it struggling and suffering.

Now, when you "build communion" you look for a father figure. There is such a thing as an unhealthy dependence. A father can be a tyrant and a despot, or a loving father, it makes no difference. Well, of course it makes a difference. But in either case, minority, dependence on a father, is something to get over, something to outgrow. You can't stay locked up in dependence all your life. But then again there is a dependence, and a fatherhood, that is positive. And this dependence and fatherhood are necessary in order to be a human being. I don't know if I'm right, but I think that one of the forces that thrusts human beings to sacrifice themselves for others, thrusts them to unselfishness, is the force of the child-father relationship.

Basically you're here with me, Pedro, to try to understand your life and live it because you've been thrust here by a problem of fatherhood. How often you've told me that you love your father but you can't accept him the way he is! This is the gist of all of our conversations. You're looking for a different relationship, a new relationship with your father. Now, those who live their lives and direct their activity in the way we call revolutionary, because they don't accept society as it is—aren't they perhaps looking for a new father figure?

There's a Mexican writer who says the Mexicans are an orphaned people. Are we not *all* orphans in search of a father? Those who think they've found him—who think their living earthly father is all they need, or who spend their lives reminiscing about their departed father—are buried in the past, are adult babies. They are the ones who fight to keep society the way it is, and fill the air with a stench like that of dead animals. If we read the gospel against the "background music" of a world in need of change, we understand this. Otherwise we don't. Jesus speaks of a father as someone to be found, someone whom we must discover in a constant quest for communion. Surely you have heard the beautiful text, Pedro, in chapter five of Saint Matthew:

> Love your enemies, pray for your persecutors. This will prove that you are sons of your heavenly Father, for his sun

rises on the bad and the good, he rains on the just and the unjust [vv. 44–45].

We could analyze these words, as scholars do, and yet fail to understand them. It seems to me that Jesus is saying: "Live a life that is a search for communion. Let nothing stop you. Let evil be no barrier. Overcome all obstacles. And thus you will become sons and daughters of my Father."

My love for my father, all frozen up within itself, can be a selfish love, a preoccupation with my own convenience. I don't want to leave home, it's too nice here. What's yours is mine, says the father in Saint Luke's famous chapter 15, the story of the prodigal. The quest for communion, the determination to build a community of brothers and sisters cost what it may, is acknowledgment of the Father. The love that atheists have for their brothers and sisters, if it's sincere, is more religious than believers' love for their heavenly Father if their love fails to issue in unselfishness.

I was really struck, Pedro, in that rehabilitation center for drug addicts that I've told you about so many times, with the love the young persons there have for one another—their gentleness, their sensitivity, as they help one another, lend personal objects, or speak together. And all of them, every last one of them, eventually find their father—their skid-row alcoholic father, frequently, or the father who deserted their family, or who was such a tyrant. And nearly all of them, after a while at the center, go back home on their own, to speak "man to man" with their fathers, fearlessly. They feel strong. What makes them so strong? What's their support, their mainstay? It's the fellowship, the communion, the community they've found at that center! They're strong in the discovery of the force that their fathers may never have really found: love and friendship. They feel a mighty call to rehabilitate the image of their father. And no one issues this challenge. It's like a law that springs up as a normal, logical consequence of the new life experience they've found. Fatherhood is seen, and reconstructed, from brotherhood and sisterhood, *not vice versa*. Do you see, Pedro, how the gospel fits in perfectly with the deepest and truest laws of the human person? The gospel guides us not toward the destruction of our being, but toward the genuine growth of our being. I don't know how far philosophical anthropology and experimental psychology have gotten along these lines. But I've discovered from experience that the gospel is the truth.

In a Communion of Brothers and Sisters: Love

Let's read Matthew 25, Pedro. That's the key. Jesus is answering a question there that has always been a problem: How can we serve God? We feel that we ought to be answering this question with our very lives. It's a responsibility we can't escape. And those who try to escape, wrecking their own happiness as they wreck that of others, are only one more proof that this is a real responsibility. This is no nightmare of a tortured, guilt-ridden mind! Jesus' answer is simple. Build communion where communion has been abolished. Fill the communion void. "I was hungry and you gave me food, I was thirsty and you gave me drink. I was a stranger and you welcomed me" (Matt. 25:35).

From one point of view, there's only one way to feed the hungry. From another point of view, there are different ways. For example, families march in Caracas to protest eviction from their neighborhoods and homes. This is a statement of the right of every citizen to have a place to live. If we were in a position to help them, by marching with them, and paying all the consequences—the tear gas, the beatings, jail, and all the nice things that happen to those who demand their rights—this would be "welcoming strangers." To demand that villagers be received and heard when they go to the dispensary, and to demand that the physician devote his time to visiting the sick instead of playing cards, and visit them conscientiously—all this is "visiting the sick." Society evolves in two directions: what at one time passes for "charity" eventually becomes legislated as obligation. And love shifts from the individual sphere to the collective, political sphere.

Do you understand what I mean, Pedro? I mean that at the time of Saint Vincent de Paul—about three hundred years ago—when someone with a terminal disease had no money, he or she had to die in abandonment, without any help of any kind. To help such persons in any way, so that they would not just die in the gutter, was considered an act of charity. Today, if you find out there's somebody like Patricio, sick in bed for six years, you march to city hall along with everyone else to protest, because the civil authorities haven't done their duty. After all, one of the duties of public officials is to care for the sick. Do you remember, when we had a meeting to stage a protest, how somebody said, "This party we elected promised to be a 'party of the people,' but now that the election's over, the poor are abandoned as always"? The help we give Patricio by marching on city hall so he can get the medical help he needs is a political act.

Today, homeless families living on the outskirts of big cities number in the thousands. Suppose you take one of these families into your own home. Is the overall problem solved? No. The evil continues. Now, suppose instead we were all to get together so they could have a place to live, and water to drink, and all the necessities of life? That would be a more effective way of "taking in" these homeless families.

Of course, there's a serious danger in all this, Pedro, and we have to be careful about it. It's the danger of losing sight of the person. Anyone who gets involved in politics, even on the "good side," runs the risk of regarding persons as statistics, and losing a sense of the human, the personal—which we must never lose sight of, in any of our decisions. Patricio is undoubtedly pleased that all his neighbors are concerned about him and go to town to protest. He feels the solidarity of his fellow workers. The fact that Ramón Gamboa goes to play cards with him every evening and keep him company is also a form of love, of fellowship, which we must not look down on just because "today's world calls for deep, radical changes," even though that statement is of course true. The warmth of love and friendship, the capacity to understand what others need, are as necessary for life as medicine and monthly welfare checks. The Christian has the duty of being an obstacle to society's transforming itself into a mechanized chicken farm, where all the pullets are vaccinated, well fed, and bathed in an odor of hygiene. At the same time, in order to discharge our duty as Christians, we must be careful not to shut ourselves up within our little pet "charities." And we must be careful not to call it "charity"—a widely misused word—when something is a matter of pure justice.

I'd like to go back to a point we left suspended, Pedro—the one about recovering fatherhood by means of "building communion." In Matthew 25, those who serve Jesus by serving their neighbor find their way to the Father: "Come, you have my Father's blessing! Inherit the kingdom prepared for you from the creation of the world" (v. 34). The Father is the creator of the world, the creator of life. But any fatherhood of dependency must be burst asunder and reexplored, in order to attain to an "acquired" fatherhood. These are difficult words and concepts, Pedro, but what I mean is this. Fatherhood becomes collective, communitarian, instead of individualistic. I discover the father in the company of my sisters and brothers and because of my sisters and brothers. The horizontal vector leads to the vertical. I wish I could explain this to everyone who has such a fear of "horizontalism," a fear that religion will be evacuated of its true content if too much attention is paid to one's neighbor at one's side, the persons on the horizontal plane with oneself. These Christians would rather concentrate on the "vertical" plane, the axis running up and down, the axis of adoration and prayer extending from earth the heaven, to God, "up there" in glory. And I'd like to tell all these "verticalists," as such Christians might be called, how we rediscover true fatherhood, the fatherhood of God—as "vertical" as you please—precisely through the horizontal, through my brothers and sisters. But it's a waste of time.

When verticalists claim to have found the Father, but keep everything for themselves, and remain individualistic, closed up in themselves, then they've found the concept of paternity we all start out with, that of the father who fails to save them from fear because he simply keeps them clutched tight in his arms amidst a dark and threatening world. No, if there's such a thing as a positive, essential fatherhood, it's not the fatherhood we start out with, but the fatherhood we end up with in the achievement of a communion of brothers and sisters. The negative father must be fled, must be rehabilitated. We must be delivered, liberated from him. The more you distance yourself from your father, Pedro, throwing yourself into this struggle to build communion in the world, and losing yourself in this struggle, the nearer you come to him, to the true encounter with him. I have had this experience personally, and now I'm living it again with you, and with so many other young persons.

Jesus' statement, "As often as you did it for one of my least brothers, you did it for me" (Matt. 25:40) is still not very clear to you, Pedro. You think Jesus meant the service done to a poor person today is really being done to Jesus *instead* of to the poor person whom you see in front of you, as if the flesh-and-blood poor person need not be really very important to a Christian. Christians need not concern themselves with Carlos, Ramón, and Patricio. What is important is the One standing behind them, Jesus—and especially, the reward the Christian is to receive for serving Jesus through Carlos, Ramón, and Patricio.

It's true, Pedro, that many a Christian thinks this. But what is the real meaning of Jesus' words? As you know, I'm not an expert on the Bible, but it seems clear to me that what Jesus means is: God, who is the Absolute, the One with whom you seek to communicate, will never be found apart from Carlos, Ramón, and Patricio. Obviously, these three are not God. But we are looking for the Absolute, and we are journeying toward the Absolute, in successive relationships, first through a relationship with Carlos, Ramón, and Patricio, and then with God in and through them. It is in human relationships that the Absolute becomes present and accessible.

Paradise

What is paradise? It is reaching the point at which we aspire to arrive. It is the point at which we feel and know we are loved—the truest need that each of us has within us. We cannot give love unless we receive it. The more consistently we try to create communion, the more we are daughters and sons of the Father.

Paradise is not a private pavilion somewhere, a first-class compartment reserved for "the good." It is in and through communion with our brothers and sisters that we discover the Father. Communion with them and communion with the Father are not two separate things. In communion with our fellow human beings we discover that love is one, springing from a single source and circulating and brightening and engulfing all the decisions that we make to build communion in the world.

I hope you understand what I mean, Pedro. We're brothers and sisters because we're sons and daughters of the same Father, and we become sons and daughters of the Father in our quest for communion with our brothers and sisters. We cannot begin to love unless we have received a bit of love—unless we have an initial impetus.

Beginning with this initial thrust, in response to the force that inspires us to give our lives to the building of communion with our sisters and brothers, we immerse ourselves ever deeper into the Father's love.

5

Strike for the Root

As long as we're on the subject of love—maybe I should go back and talk about the love of a couple for one another, the love of a man and a woman.

First let me explain how the different "anthropologies" of today—the different theories of the human being—lead to the gospel. Every person or group of persons who develops a general theory of reality are obliged to include a theory of the human being, are obliged to state how they think of the human person, how they see the human person. Very briefly, here is what today's theories have said about the human being: that it is in the condition of a creature—that is, is dependent, a being destined for death— that is, headed for the point of perfect knowing, and that point is death. Marxism sees human beings in a certain relationship. It cannot see them apart from that relationship. Human beings find themselves enmeshed in a structure that makes them what they are at the moment, but they can change the structure and thereby profoundly modify their being. Men and women can change the structures of society from structures of dependence and oppression to structures of equality.

All of today's anthropologies or conceptions of the human being agree on one thing: they all see the human being as a being in need of liberation, and moving toward liberation. Whether impelled by the terror of death, or by the ideal of justice, or by the need to break out of a dependency—one way or another, the human being is on the move.

I have to say, Pedro, that the anthropology I find the least convincing is the one followed by the great majority of Catholics. Concerned to preserve a permanent principle, a treasure given to us by God that we are to safeguard, Catholics often feel that they've "already arrived." And so they do not participate in this laborious quest for a new humankind. This is nothing new. When Jesus says, "The truth will set you free" (John 8:32), there is pandemonium. What? Will set us free? But we're already free! We're slaves to nobody. And there is such a commotion that the scene threatens to end in catastrophe.

I have become convinced that Catholics—not all of them, but too many of them—want to feel secure. Freedom? We already have it. Why speak to us of liberation? We *are* children of the Father— what do you mean, "*become* children of the Father"?

The human being is a relationship?, they ask. But a person isn't a relationship, a person is an absolute, something in itself, a projection, reflection, of an infinite and absolute Being. Why should we feel ourselves to be in a relationship? After all, yesterday as today, Jesus seeks his own thing among those who have no fear of losing, among those whose way of life is such that they don't even think about insecurity.

You see, Pedro, I have a very simple view of life. I know it costs something to be consistent with this simplicity. The human being is someone in quest of communion, someone in the process of the creation of communion. The human being is a being in the process of emerging from its own "I," the process of bursting the barriers of the past, and rediscovering fatherhood.

The blood circulating within us and the love that drives us onward is the Father's love. I once thought that human love par excellence was sexual love. And today I'm still convinced that sexual love is extremely important. But today I would add something to what I wrote some years ago, some qualifications that now seem to me to be essential. *In the encounter between woman and man, these two love each other with the only love they have—the Father's love.* It's not a love reborn from the discovery of a love for their brothers and sisters, not a love sprung from the toil of building communion, but a love sprung from the love that comes from flesh and blood.

I don't want to be quoting the Bible all the time, Pedro, and notice that your friends don't go around with copies of the Bible, but I'd like you to listen to what it says on our subject in the first chapter of Saint John:

> Any who did accept him he empowered to become children of God . . . who were begotten not by blood, nor by carnal desire, nor by man's willing it, but by God [vv. 12–13].

Now we're in a position to understand this seeming contradiction: we *are* children of God already, and we are to *become* children of God. Catholics too often stop with the first half. "We *are* children of God. We *are* children of Abraham." Their thinking has been corrupted by a certain philosophy of being that is static, stationary, frozen. And it continues to be the basis of Catholic education. I realize that many of them simply cannot accept both poles of this dynamic tension simultaneously: we *are* the daughters and sons of God, and we must *become* such.

To get back to the couple. Man and woman approach one another in the flesh-and-blood love of the father. All the wild elements of their love run together in a turbulent expression of the dynamics of fatherhood. In poor families, sex tends to be brutal. In a family of the bourgeois type, protectionism and egotism prevail: "I give you everything you need. You shall lack for nothing. I give you the best, you have the right to everything."

I remember the story of a young bourgeois woman who married, had children, and everything was going swimmingly—when suddenly, at about thirty years of age, her husband died. The young woman had the whole town at her feet, offering her consolation. But she was inconsolable. Her mother had Masses said and scoured the countryside for faith-healers to help her poor daughter survive such a disaster. The whole town spoke of nothing but poor Luisa and what had happened to her. I remember what one of her friends said: "She had everything. This was the first time in her life she had ever heard 'no.' "

The middle class lives in this facile dependency, Pedro, in this individualism. The boy or girl who comes from the common people feels orphaned, kicked out of the house. There is a kind of international union of youth in our times, a bond of unity among the increasing number of "orphaned" youth. The womb-family is becoming less and less common.

The man-woman encounter generally takes place at this level of unliberated love, and this is why sexual love is so full of aggressivity and possessiveness. The dances and the folklore of all the countries that I've visited depict love as abduction, rape. In all languages, to say, "I've done it to you, I've caught you," a vulgar expression for copulation is used. In parts of Mexico they use the word *singar,* meaning to "skin" somebody, or to "cut off the tail." It's used as a noun, too, for the parsley that goes in all the sauces. Originally it meant rape. It's an expression of male sastisfaction. "I've had you, I've made you, I've done it to you." Life is thought of as successful domination: "Finally I've mastered you." And fatherhood is conceived in terms of dependency.

We feel driven from one conception of fatherhood to the other. We could get stuck in the first, where fatherhood is rape, because it's more convenient. Or, in this stage, we can yearn for freedom. If we stay with the first stage, the rape stage, we block our quest for our own being, and we can put on a masquerade, but we shall never be authentic. As it happens, the one law of life has three aspects: identity, communion, and new fatherhood. That is, we are authentic if we break out of dependence on our father, for the adventure of communion—and then rebuild, in this adventure, the relationship with our father. Basically this is the structure of liberation.

When we leave the problem of love unresolved, when we fail to confront the adventure of communion courageously, we cover our nakedness, our failure, with two false masks—both seemingly very thick and solid, but in reality flimsy and tenuous as the morning mist: money and power. And a raving existence is born, violence against the weakest, all our attention concentrated on the effort to reach the top of the heap. Little by little we renounce the effort to build communion, we renounce any hope of love and friendship and the taste for them, and become accustomed to the taste for dominating others. The society we live in is violent and competitive—two complementary faces of a pesonality that has lost its true reason for being.

Liberation in Personal Relationships

Today, Pedro, you told me something, in your own words, that made me leap for joy. You've discovered that, almost instinctively, you've forbidden yourself all the things that would have made you a loser. You've said no to marijuana, to the bordello, and to so many other things you could have had. You said, "I knew I was going to have to live with myself all my life. Friends change, but I'm with myself all my life." This is your way of expressing your identity, Pedro.

Everyone wants to be who they are, and this is healthy. They all seek the things that make them grow, and renounce what paralyzes their growth. One of my favorite authors, Pierre Teilhard de Chardin, speaks of the forces of growth and the forces of "diminishment." Love is a growth force, and the only growth force, but what is ordinarily meant by love can actually destroy us.

A man burdens a woman with his own life burden, from which he has never become free himself: dependence—the other face of ownership. Marxists maintain that this "proprietary instinct" is the product of a capitalistic society. Others hold that a capitalistic society arises from the proprietary instinct, and that when private property is eliminated this instinct turns toward domination of both women and men as property. And there are indeed socialist societies where "despotism"—the itch to command and subject and be obeyed—seems to be as rife as anywhere else in the world.

In making this criticism I am not drawing the conclusion that it is useless to change the world, because "human beings will always be human beings." I shall never tire of warning you, Pedro, that such a conclusion is "tendentious"—slanted and prejudiced. We must never accept it. What we need to do is fight all forms of domination and "ownership"—and of authoritarianism, which is the same thing—in whatever form they present themselves.

When we hear of "masculine responsibility," meaning a responsibility to dominate, we should realize that this attitude is a masculine disease, and one that infects women too. This is fatherhood gone insane, and women can suffer from the same insanity. What does "boss" mean? It means big fat daddy, false father, father with a stick in his hand. But women can be bosses, too. You have it in your literature, Pedro, in the novel *Doña Barbara*, which is the story of a young girl who is raped, but who sees, in a sudden flash one day, that love is possible. Do you remember Asdrubal in that novel? He is the light in the dark, who offers the prospect of a love of equals, a love between companions, without domination by either party. But their love becomes impossible, and Doña Barbara becomes a devourer of men—a "boss." Against their destructive, wild genital thrust she sets a magical destructive power of her own. And both, woman and man, are caught in this magic circle of "fatherly" love, unremade in the communion of sister and brother. Both fall short of communion—never take the leap—and are caught in a series of provisional, successive satisfactions.

By this I mean a satisfaction that is not sought in growth, but in the repetition of the same acts. In other words, persons make no effort to be today what they were not yesterday, take no pleasure in advancement, but seek their satisfaction in the endless repetition of the same thing. Alcoholics get into a circle they can't get out of: thirst-satisfaction-frustration, then the frustration combines with and compounds a new thirst, and the victims are caught in the circle for good.

I agree with the socialists. It's time to destroy the structures. When you are harassed by a swarm of wasps, you go looking for the nest, and you destroy it. But the wasps survive. They simply build a nest somewhere else. So the only thing to do is destroy the wasps. To apply the parable: it's fine to destroy the structures, but human beings will remain the same, so you'll have to destroy them. God, however, does not wish their death, but rather their conversion, and their rebaptism in fellowship and communion.

The more I find myself free of individualism, the more clearly I see that there's no use fighting on the human being's interior front alone. *We can be liberated only in our relationships.* It is of no importance whether human beings exist in themselves prescinding from their relationships. Liberation is the liberation of personal relationships. Let me explain what I mean.

You can see whether a man is the subject of a liberation process, Pedro, by examining his relationships with women, with his friends, and with the political community. Such a relationship is not "good or bad"; it moves toward the better or toward the worse. In gospel terms, it moves toward light or toward darkness. Remember, Pedro, persons, like society, are to move from slavery toward freedom—then from freedom toward a greater freedom. The person who refuses to accept things as they are, does not retreat in the face of suffering, inconvenience, or anything else that comes as a result of life in movement.

Christian training and education, especially in the past, was directed toward the molding of a human being as perfect as a flawless Greek statue. Its symbol was the white garment, absolutely stainless. The human being was not seen in terms of relationships with others. I remember one time when I had said this in public, the young persons present understood, but one older man—not so old chronologically, but old in his mentality— vigorously protested. Perhaps you're right, Pedro, perhaps I could have said it a little more gently. But I'm so sensitive to individualistic, cerebral education, which I eventually found out had nothing to do with the gospel, that I feel like being very forthright about it.

The Body as a Means of Communion

Pedro, let's read your favorite passage—Mark 10, Jesus' encounter with the rich young man. Do you remember what we have here? The young man is a good person, but he's missing something, and he goes in search of advice as to what he ought to do. Jesus tells him, simply, that it's not enough to be good. You have to be able to *love.* What you're missing, my friend, is involvement in a relationship with others. It's as if Jesus were saying, "You're a good fellow. You're ready for life. At Pharisee College you'd win a prize. You haven't abandoned yourself to vices, you've saved yourself, preserved yourself. Now come down to the battlefield and start fighting. Sell what you have, give the proceeds to the poor, and come after me."

But this page fell into the hands of priests and nuns, and they've given it a different meaning. "As a Christian of the masses, of the lowest degree—you're fine. But you belong to the Christian proletariat. Would you like to go first class? Would you like to enter the House of Lords? Go, sell what you have, give the proceeds to the poor, and come after me."

Pedro, you have no idea how much hair-splitting has been done over this passage from the gospel. May the young man tell the Lord no? Is what Jesus asks of him obligatory, or not? If he says no, will he be saved? Christians originally took sides against any class division of society. But in my interpretation of this passage I've introduced classes into the gospel! I've marked off the boundaries of the little garden where only a few may enter, and distinguished it from the great field where everyone else stands. It's like the "gardens of peace," the cemeteries of the poor, and those of the rich. And in this year of grace 1986 the offices of the church continue to tend the cemeteries of the rich. What "revolution" are they expecting, an atomic one, a meteorological one? Let's read this passage from the gospel on another wavelength. "My son, you're fine, you look like a good person. Well, then, what are you waiting for? Put your hand on the plow, and come work with me. We'll build the reign of God, a more just society, a community of brothers and sisters. Start getting rid of your money. That's the main obstacle. You can't preach justice if you're rooted in injustice. Theologians of coming centuries will teach you this." I think it's fair to say that the gospel never speaks of a perfect individual apart from a context of his or her relationships of communion. You become perfect by building communion. This is the key to everything.

The problem of love between man and woman is a matter of relationship? What a discovery! Well, yes, it's nothing new. But we'll come back to this discovery later, to try to understand more about relationships.

Here is the key to the problem of chastity, which we've touched on a few times in passing. Chastity is the use of the body and sexuality in such a way that this use will build communion, not discord, not separation. We've seen that goods can be used in such a way as to cause either communion or separation. So too your sexuality can be used to dominate, to make yourself and your partner less of a person—or to build communion, a community.

In this perspective, we have to distinguish a repressive chastity from an expressive chastity. Repressive chastity is one that is all closed up in a circle of individualism. Young persons are taught "chastity" as a kind of training exercise—what we used to call "self-mastery," as when you might want to get somebody not to smoke or drink so as not to scatter the energy they'll need to be a good athlete, or a good "Aloysius Gonzaga under glass." It was like a man watching his money and not "wasting it on women."

Psychology has connected this kind of "chastity" with the interior violence necessary for a capitalistic society. Love of money, of competition, of possessions, fascism as one's outlook on life—these are the fruits of sexual repression. Anything that shuts the individual off from others, anything tending to isolate and "distance" a person from a communion of brothers and sisters as the true ideal, is a deadly poison. Chastity, as it has actually been promoted and instilled, has served to form the fascist. Of this there can be no doubt.

Yes, Pedro, for me a "fascist" is a person on guard against others, a person who does not look on others with a look of love and trust, but who regards them as individuals to be "put into line" and forced to obey.

Yes, there are fascists in religious communities, in political parties, in all human structures. And it would appear that repressed sexual energy is very convenient when it comes to making fascists. Evangelical chastity is not repression. Simply put, it is making your very body available for the building of communion. The couple should be the ultimate, the most perfect, symbol of communion and friendship.

This isn't the way it is in the world we live in, but it is what evangelization should aim at as the ideal. I'm in agreement with those who are against chastity when it's repressive, when it becomes a person's path to solitude. Is it possible to reach such a degree of liberation, Pedro, that your sexuality actually becomes a quest for communion and friendship? Well, you've made one discovery on your own: the more you feel yourself to be in the service of the kingdom, the more you're freed from the notion of women as sex objects. I'm very pleased with your discovery. But I would be remiss if I failed to warn you against placing too much confidence in yourself.

Never forget what Jesus said about chastity: that it's impossible for human beings, and possible only for God. So don't concentrate too much on the "strength" necessary to resist evil. Concentrate on the transformation occurring within you, concentrate on how you're becoming a new human being, capable of communion. Human liberation that isn't total isn't liberation. Those who struggle for justice can be unjust themselves—you can see it in their interpersonal relationships.

We can move in the direction of justice, but if our personal relationships don't become more human, we haven't moved in the direction of the reign of God, and in the long run we'll discover that our point of arrival is just another form of tyranny. As Christians we must not fear to stand up for this principle in revolutionary circles when we hear that a human being counts for nothing or that personal problems are "bourgeois." Don't weaken. The man who oppresses women, or who can't get along with his friends, will fail to make his revolution a true liberation.

Pedro, I'd like to talk to you a little bit about chastity from the viewpoint of a celibate. You understand what chastity means for you and your friends—for persons you call "normal." For most persons chastity will be a matter of using their sexuality in such a way as to build a communion of brothers and sisters, and not to increase the number of persons in the world who are simply used and thrown away like so many Coke cans. It's a matter of using their sexuality in such a way as not simply to multiply the number of children generated, as animals generate litters, but procreated by couples clear-sighted and creative in their communion.

But what point is there in priests and nuns? What point is there in persons who don't get married? You apologized, Pedro, and explained you didn't mean me, because as we've been living together here you've seen a "whole slew of reasons" for celibacy. But excuse me, Pedro—aren't those rather utilitarian reasons? I've often met persons who've told me they understand sisters in hospitals or orphanages. How would they be able to do what they're doing if they had families of their own? This justification of celibacy is utilitarian, and false. Married persons can devote themselves to orphans, or the elderly, or the infirm, too.

No, for me there's a deeper meaning in this consecration to God for the sake of the kingdom. Your body becomes a sign of communion, a sign of a total gift of yourself to others without taking anything back for yourself. You're repeating what Christ did. He didn't give us things, words, laws—he gave us his body, to unite us, to be communion among us.

A person who accepts celibacy by "vocation"—that is, in response to an intuition that is very hard to explain in words—and lives it in fidelity, will be recognizable from the result: a chaste person is not a repressed person. Chastity and repression are two entirely different things. A person who has renounced the genital expression of sexuality should make others feel more communion, more freedom. In the presence of a man who lives entirely for the reign of God, a woman should sense a love that doesn't frighten, a love that is not in any way a violation of her person. I can't help but think of the Samaritan woman, who opened out to our Lord so completely, so fearlessly, and felt loved in a new way—a way she'd never known till that moment.

You see, Pedro, some persons—all too few, actually—make you so happy to see them that they just seem to give you gladness, like Elisa who came to see us the other day and you said it was as if our shack were "all lighted up or something." Somehow you know it's a good thing that these persons aren't married. But when you run into an aggressive, authoritarian, selfish person, interested only in hobbies, who strokes the hood of his car as if it were a young woman's cheek, or somebody all full of fears, then celibacy repels you.

Celibacy remains a mystery. I don't think God is any more pleased with a celibate than with a married person. God is pleased with the person who does a better job of building a communion of brothers and sisters, building the reign of God. The person closest to God is surely the one who is better at fellowship and communion.

There are persons called "solitaries"—hermits—who withdraw from the world in search of God. They have to be sure they aren't doing this just to have a peaceful life, or to serve God as some sort of special courtier before the divine throne. God doesn't need this. It has to be because they're torn to pieces inside by human dividedness, by the absence of a communion of sisters and brothers, and they think that their fervent prayers, their groans of anguish rising to the Father, will contribute to peace and communion. This is the only way they make any sense. Otherwise, instead of being disciples of Christ they'll be some sort of sons and daughters of Plato.

To get back to our conversation about celibacy—which certainly hasn't been very enlightening for you so far, Pedro—I'd say that celibacy proclaims three messages. First, that God is absolute. God can ask anything of me. And as a matter of fact we believe that the intuition we've had not to marry comes from God. Secondly, that the liberation to which all human beings aspire is the rebirth of a relationship, the transformation-in-depth of the human relationship. Thirdly, that this communion comes by way of the body. It's not an "idealistic" communion. The body must become a means of communion, not division. Let's go back to a point we were on when we were talking about the Eucharist. Communion among us doesn't bypass the body. It comes precisely by way of the body.

This is as far as we'll go with this for now. The body is a means of liberation somehow. To understand this subject more deeply, we'll have to be further along the road to liberation.

A Society of Friends

Let's see whether we can shed a little light on a certain word. We often see it in the newspapers, and I've been using it to sum up lots of things. It's the word "fascism."

Fascism is a political movement that sprang up in Italy and Germany. But I've been using the word in a much broader sense. When I say "fascist" I mean anyone who has no confidence in human beings—someone who is afraid of human beings. Persons are your enemies. You'd better watch out for them. And there are three ways to keep them in line: violence, authority, and benefaction.

You can find the fascist spirit anywhere. Basically it's the spirit of the tycoon, of the rich. They couldn't have arrived where they are if they had confidence in human nature! The fascist will always tell you that human beings are an ignorant, perverse lot, and that you have to treat them like children. And if you look at the way human communities are, the fascists might seem to be right!

But fascism is a shortcut. Fascism dangles a "quick fix" in front of you, an immediate, radical solution. But being a shortcut, a detour, it throws a roadblock across the highway we should be walking, the road to liberation and fulfillment, and sends us up Fear Alley instead. And there we get stuck and the journey is over. We're riveted in individualism now, and individualism glues us to that perilous paternalistic dependency of which I've spoken so much.

Communion-building goes slowly and painfully. It's a road full of potholes. It's enough to discourage anyone! But it's the only human road. It's our condition. A group of persons held together by fear and authoritarianism can't be a community of brothers and sisters. Fear, mutual mistrust, flattery of authority to keep in its good graces—this whole unhealthy atmosphere is antigospel. Why does it happen especially in "religious" groups? Because religion and religious life, instead of being presented as a breach, a breaking-free, is presented as a refuge, an escape. " 'Come after me. . . .' They immediately *abandoned their nets* and became his followers" (Mark 1:17–18). But where can you find this outside the gospel?

Fascist conduct is not a free and voluntary choice. It's the constrained behavior of an unfree person. Liberation is "communion and fellowship"—that is, trust in human beings, a set of relationships among equals. Unliberation is diffidence, subordination, violence. Anyone not on the road to liberation is forced to be a fascist. And Pedro, this is why persons, and peoples, are more disposed to fascism than to fully human relationships. Only the Spirit of the Lord can "fill the land" with this liberty, this freedom.

One of the signs, in fact the main sign, of a person of the kingdom, a person on the road to freedom, is that he or she is against all fascisms, struggling to make all forms of political, religious, and familial fascism disappear from the face of the earth. I can't claim to be free if I'm not struggling for the liberation of my sisters and brothers, if I'm not struggling for the establishment of the ideal of freedom in the world. Building communion, building a community of brothers and sisters, means building freedom. The roots of fascism and freedom are in a person's heart. I'd even say that we're all born fascists and must become Christians.

Pedro, do you remember the day we talked about capitalists who fence off their property with barbed wire? And you asked whether anyone could break through this barbed wire. Well, I see the time has come to talk to you about how I see Jesus.

6

Reading the Gospel in Life

In coming to live with us, Jesus not only gave us communion-building as our only task, telling us that in this way we would be sons and daughters of his Father—he also put a galvanizing force into the world, into history. He won't leave us in peace till we walk this road. But we are always putting up so strong a resistance that it seems as if the world were headed toward fascism and individualism. Then the decentralizing force emanating from Jesus rends persons on the inside, obliging them to emerge from themselves. We call it grace. It is present in the concrete circumstances of life. Those who refuse to obey it are alienated for good and all.

Different kinds of experiences can serve to make you emerge from yourself and hurl you into this adventure of building a communion of sisters and brothers—a death, a great sorrow, holding public office, being in the hands of the police for days with a hood over your head—but it's always one and the same grace, the grace to emerge from yourself, the grace to notice that others are there. For a rich person, someone accustomed to see others as a means to personal advantage, the center of gravity doesn't shift all that easily. But let's be filled with confidence! God has put this force in the world and it's impossible for negative forces, the forces of death, to overcome it.

Jesus has told us that the gates of hell will never prevail against his church. This promise serves as a pretext for certain persons, who feel themselves to be in "their church" as in some kind of citadel, simply to keep on sleeping peacefully. But this citadel can be brought down, its walls can be razed. Jerusalem and its temple were razed. But the church as a gathering of sisters and brothers, the church as human communion, will infallibly endure.

From this point of view you can say that true revolutions are the ones that take humanity a step forward in the direction of freedom, and that freedom is a common relationship of brothers and sisters. This book you see me reading, Pedro (José Comblin, *Théologie de la révolution*, 1970) tells of four great revolutions motivated by a quest for liberty and freedom—for the freedom of the church from political society, the freedom of individuals to believe and profess their faith as they see fit, the freedom of the citizen (that is, the right of the individual vis-à-vis society), and socialistic freedom, which refuses to allow labor and production to be deeds of slavery but insists they become deeds of freedom.

All this is too much to explain in just a few words, of course, but we understand each other, Pedro, because we're in continual dialogue. When I was your age I went to college, and the focal point of our study was the work of Georg Wilhelm Friedrich Hegel. Now, at this same moment, it so happened, I came to grasp that Jesus had brought the leaven of liberation into the world and that this is why humanity is so restless: because it has this thing to develop from now on, endlessly. Revolutions aren't Christian, I said to myself; and you don't have to know much about the church to know that it's antirevolutionary, or to see the panic on the faces of churchmen today with regard to communism.

And I can't deny it, Pedro. The institutional church in antirevolutionary. But the soul of genuine revolution is evangelical. Here human beings are being stirred by the absolute need for freedom. We aren't born free. We gain our freedom. Not everything that happens in a revolution is evangelical, of course. Is an assault on a bank, or torture, or the kidnapping of an industrialist evangelical? It's evangelical to move in the direction of freedom.

Could the unfree have some other way of accomplishing their liberation? I think they could, and we Christians must invent it. But the new way won't be by washing our hands of the problem. "You can't have revolutions without bloodshed. So let's don't have one. Let's leave things as they are. Let's keep on sleeping." That would be like saying, "Some foods are poisonous. So let's not eat." History creates social needs, tensions, and these needs and tensions make revolutions inevitable. Clichés like, "violence breeds violence," "peace is the highest good," "lose peace and lose all"— these have never had any influence on history. They're pure rhetoric.

As long as we're on the subject, Pedro, I'd like to mention this: there's a substantial difference between those who perform acts of violence or war in behalf of liberty, and those who commit these same acts to slow down or halt the march of history. It's the difference between the surgeon who operates on your stomach and the murderer who plunges a knife into your belly. When the moment of revolution is over, when the dust of violence settles, the masses call those who have fought for liberty heroes and martyrs. But the reactionaries they call butchers.

I was saying this to an Argentinian—a good Catholic, and a fine torturer, a member of an antisubversive group. "We're sacrificing ourselves for our country," he told me. "Well," I retorted, "the day will come when the president of Argentina will pay a state visit to a statue of Che Guevara, and the cardinal archbishop of Buenos Aires will sprinkle it with holy water. But you can be sure you'll never have your statue up anywhere. Butchers never get one."

Today nearly all Christians acknowledge that the deep inspiration of the French Revolution was actually evangelical. It won't be long—you'll still be living, Pedro—before you'll be hearing that the inspiration of the Marxist or socialist revolution is evangelical.

There's an important difference between these two kinds of violence and violent persons. Revolutionary violence is humane. It respects the human person. The true revolutionary is a human being who loves, who is moved by love. The butcher is inhuman. The butcher does not battle for the human being.

Revolutionaries have caught a glimpse of the land of promise. Their journey toward this land is firmly motivated by love, though they may be mistaken in their means. Counterrevolutionaries are unwilling to budge. They refuse to move from the ground underfoot. They seek to destroy all who oppose their self-proclaimed rights. You have to get your thinking straight before you know which side a follower of Christ should be on. When the battle is done, many Christians look about and find themselves surrounded by mummies.

The second thing I want to tell you, Pedro, is that I can see the idea of freedom growing ever clearer in history, sinking ever deeper roots in history. Our Christian culture has gone through four revolutions. The first was the church's revolt against the Roman empire. This is when we pitched camp. Now we had a base to move from in our struggle to gain the freedom of daughters and sons of God, the freedom to move toward God. And this was our second revolution. Then, thirdly, we won the freedom of citizenship. Now every person was basically equal to every other. Finally, we are changing at their roots the relationships of production, the use of goods, so that goods will no longer generate a relationship of employer and slave, but a relationship of equality, of fellowship. The theme of freedom is the theme of the human-being-as-such as the agent of legislation, then the human being in society, and finally human beings in communion with one another and with nature.

This is just a rough sketch, of course. A revolution is not something you can put your finger on. You can't guide and control the whole process of a revolution from beginning to end. You see only that a revolution launches an attack on a certain situation—a situation that demands a human reaction, such an urgent imperative that it explodes.

Revolution is made by a people. But at the same time it is thrust on a people. The moment comes, and you can't "put it off till tomorrow." You can't decide that it would be more convenient to have the revolution next summer instead. You can't even say that the revolution will completely solve everything. Revolutions scheduled for a certain moment of a certain day in a certain month are military revolutions. We have lots of them in Latin America. These aren't real revolutions. A revolution is like a cry, it's a problem opening up and spilling out on the floor right in front of everybody. I'd say it's like a generalization of a problem that at first only a few persons see. The principles of the French Revolution are generally accepted now, and they torment well-nigh everyone. But they haven't been put into full effect yet.

Creating a Community of Sisters and Brothers

There's a lot of truth in what they say about how much calmer the people would be if it weren't for the rabble-rousers, the ones who stir the people up. But Pedro, doesn't it seem to you that it's a duty to help a people become aware of its state of oppression, the injustice it suffers, and the opportunity for liberation? Undeniably, hatred sometimes works its way into the process of conscientization, resentment plays its part—elements, surely, of unlove. But without this "preaching," just as surely, the gospel would always be buried treasure! Today we can no longer proclaim the gospel apart from an *involvement with and among the people.*

We can read the gospel and extract principles, extract what might be called an ideology—a system for responding to the question of how we should view life and therefore how we should live. What does Jesus think of marriage? Or celibacy? Or prayer? As long as there has been a gospel, there have been theories on the gospel, and these theories, these "treatises," grew and grew. Almost right from the beginning, it was noticed that certain Greek philosophers held positions very like those of the gospel!

So the writings of the philosophers were gathered in to support the simple, naked truths of the gospel. In the process, two basic principles stand out: that the human intellect is incapable of total error, and that the gospel is tailor-made for human beings, even though it doesn't always seem to be. This is how Christian ideology came into being. Of course, the masses know this ideology only very badly, and in abridged fashion, through the preaching of their priests. Little by little this doctrine led to ramifications, and wandered a great distance from the gospel, which originally was its heart and core. And a political doctrine came into being, a doctrine of knowledge, a doctrine of art. A specialized Christian theory arose for every possible human situation.

Now, this ideology was of course in the hands of the priests, and others who had had the opportunity to study it. Pedro, you've heard it said right here in Bojó: "What can we poor ignorant persons say?" When I asked the people to comment on the parable of the sower, the reaction was unanimous: "We're not priests. We don't know." Christ had restored to them their right to speak, but the "philosophers" had intercepted and expropriated that right. Priests read all those treatises and tractates, and learn them, and so they have plenty to talk about, but they no longer speak the language of the people.

And what is happening today, especially in Latin America? New preachers have appeared. They speak of justice, of communion, of oneness, and they affirm: "You will find this in the gospel." These "truths" go directly to the people. There's not much need for explanation. And trust is born. Confidence is born, in the priests and in the church. Priests and the church have always preached truth and justice. But they have preached it in so complicated a way that we haven't understood a thing they've said.

Something is happening today like what happened in Jesus' time. The doctrine of the law had wrapped the word of God in so much ratiocination that Jesus had to peel off all the accretions and allow this word to be manifested in all its naked simplicity. This is why the scribes and the Pharisees were in such a state. Their anger with the new prophet knew no bounds.

The most important, most revolutionary of today's revolutions is the liberation of the word. The gospel can be summed up in a very simple formula: *Give glory to God by building a communion of brothers and sisters among human beings.* Today we no longer need a preacher to tell us what peace is. We need a preacher who makes peace. Christian peace is the peace proclaimed by Christ—and then rethought by Augustine, and thought again by a centuries-long chain of thinkers all the way down to a Frenchman called Jacques Maritain. To know what peace is, you'd have to read a whole library.

In Latin America the ideologues are all being put out to pasture. And the gospel is being rediscovered. The gospel can be rethought only from involvement in "communion building." Every day we must answer this question anew: Is what you are doing—the money you're spending, the persons you're meeting, and so on—is all this building communion? Or is it taking communion a step backward?

We owe the liquidation of Christian ideology to the challenge thrown at us by revolutionary movements. Of what use will it be to know who the Father is if we don't fight to be sisters and brothers? The "Christian" political parties in Latin American have fallen under this judgment. The Christian parties are Christian, but they aren't evangelical. They represent a body of political teaching, well-intentioned, doubtless, and thought out and written down by good persons. I can assure you of that: I've known a few of them. But this body of teaching is so far removed from the gospel program of a communion of brothers and sisters! Where does it bring down the mighty from their thrones and exalt the lowly? On the contrary, it makes the mighty mightier, and swells the ranks of the lowly. It would like to keep everyone in their place. Here in Latin America I think the Christian political party has finished its role in history.

The criterion by which the masses judge the priest, or the one responsible for evangelization, is whether he or she accomplishes the task of building a communion of brothers and sisters. This is never quite the same as to have studied the "tractate on marriage," or to be familiar with the latest trends in theology.

Now you see what I meant yesterday, Pedro, when I was speaking with Sister Isolina. Remember how enthusiastic she was about the sisters who went to Belgium to study catechetics? When they get back from Belgium we'll have a group of "specialists in Christianity"—for a people who no longer knows what to do with "Christianity." Workers are being sent to study silkworms in the age of nylons.

There are some persons who don't have a liberation problem, and they are content with a "community" manufactured at Mass. This is a class of persons altogether satisfied with ideology. For them the nuns from Belgium are just fine.

You ask me, Pedro, if they see this over in Rome. No. They can't see this. They realize that the masses are drifting further and further away. When persons emerge from the stage of superstition and fear, they don't want to have anything more to do with priests, or the church, or the gospel. They know this and see this over in Rome. And they are working on how to train individuals to "instruct the people." They train these "instructors" with a doctrine, a pedagogical technique, everything possible. You could give them some good advice, Pedro, because you've lived this, and are living it. But neither you nor anyone else from among the people will ever be able to advise the institutional church. The church ought to be changing the world. You know you can't drive out fear with "training." Fear is driven out by trust, by the love that means sharing, being together, living a creative friendship. Superstition is ignorance, yes; but even more so, it's *fear*—fear of God, of the saints, of the mighty, far-away church. I try to shout this at them. But I too have no "vote in the chapter room."

Until the church renounces Christianity as an ideology and believes in the gospel as the only force for liberation, as a message and force for building community, it will never reach the people. It will only supply oppressors with arms and arguments to justify and mask their injustice. The sisters from Belgium and all those like them, however poor they may be, and even though they battle for justice, are actually fomenting injustice and hindering communion.

In Europe the idea is to "evangelize" by adapting the Christian ideology to different times and cultures. In Latin America we think it more urgent to build communion and discover the gospel as the revelation of the Father who is glorified in this quest for communion. We all want the kingdom of God. But, as you see, Pedro, in practice we're divided into two apparently irreconcilable groups. Now you understand where the division is to which you've called my attention so often: there are ideological Christians and there are gospel Christians. The gospel leads you to a knowledge of truth by putting truth into practice. Ideology permits you to remain satisfied with ideas.

The battle is not between educated Christians and uneducated Christians. That would be an oversimplified, unfair way of putting it. A Christian dedicated to the building of communion can be an educated person, and in some cases must indeed know a great many things. But such a Christian does not cover over the gospel with doctoral dissertations. A Christian politician reads the gospel from a particular, concrete situation, and tries to understand it from that situation. Atheists, too, try to build fellowship, and you can sit down with them and analyze the obstacles to communion. But the gospel obliges you with a necessity so absolute, and so within you, that whatever you do seems too little. The gospel is always one step ahead of you. And you'll discover that your fellow crusaders don't always have the same love for the individual, don't always see their neighbor as sister or brother. Christians in Latin America have a great deal to do. They need not set about "educating" the people. Their task is to build the reign of God, the encounter of brothers and sisters. And this will lead to the toppling of a system that generates rivals, a system that makes and keeps equals unequal.

You ask me what I mean by this communion of fellowship, Pedro. I'd say it's the encounter, the ever truer and deeper encounter, that we seek when we reach out to help clear away everything that might present an obstacle to genuine oneness among us. What is peace? Peace is reconciliation among brothers and sisters, attained by eliminating all relationships of force, power, and superiority that are at the root of discord. Who is God? God is the Father we feel more and more as an experience of goodness and tenderness and love the more we're involved in becoming brothers and sisters to one another. Ideology will "toss off" a simple definition of what peace is, and what a world of brothers and sisters ought to be. But it maps out a project for an unreal world. Its plans are most harmonious, but they take no account of reality.

Utopia and Idealism

Let me explain to you the meaning of these two words, Pedro. You know that idealists are persons with an ideal—persons who look beyond the satisfaction of their immediate needs. This is the popular definition. And it is correct. But the term has another meaning. Idealism is a philosophical system. I won't explain it to you, because we're not interested in that right at the moment.

Ever since they started thinking, human beings have been drawn to "going beyond" the things of their immediate environment, imagining other possibilities, driven by an inner fire that enabled them to overcome the "poverty" of what they can see and touch. This evening, Pedro, you and I are in this mud hut. It's a little cold in here. There's not much light. But we can imagine ourselves in front of a fireplace in a more spacious, warm room. In other words, we can be in one place with our body and another place with our imagination. In our imagination we see hills, mountains, and starry sky overhead. And we can think of Someone who made all this, and begin to speculate whether that Someone is like ourselves, where he or she lives, and so on.

What I see gives me a little shove to go beyond my surroundings, go further, outside space and time. And I like this world of imagination and speculation, I discover analogies and ideas I've never applied to life, which could be useful in the transformation of the world.

This experience gives rise to the conviction that each of us is "two"—the Pedro who's here in this cold hut, and the Pedro who's not here but in a somewhat more pleasant sphere, wandering among the stars. We're matter and we're spirit. And the "spirit part" is regarded as clearly superior to the "matter part." Eventually the spirit comes to be thought of in terms of nobility, a kind of prince or princess, obliged to live a lowly kind of life—captured and stuck into a hole and forced to get dirty.

In the ancient world, especially in Greece, the cradle of Western philosophy, this theoretical division between soul and matter was projected into actual life. The human being, the truly human being, the one deserving to be free, was the one devoted to the activity of thinking, of writing. The truly human being, the really free one, was the intellectual. The one who worked the land or swept the streets was a slave.

I'm not giving you a lesson in history or philosophy, Pedro. I'm just trying to give you a clear picture of the influence this idealistic view has had on Christianity. When I studied the catechism I was taught that you weren't supposed to work on Sunday. But "liberal occupations" were allowed—reading, writing, drawing, working as a lawyer, and so on. What you weren't allowed to do was manual or "servile" work—cleaning shoes, sweeping, doing carpentry, blacksmith work, and so on. Today I'm ashamed that I accepted this division—work that *free* persons could do and work suitable for *slaves*. Sure, we were all sisters and brothers in Christ. And yet we accepted this division without batting an eyelash.

So when I speak of "idealism," this is how I mean it: accepting this division of human beings, and accepting the notion that the activity of thinking is superior to working with your hands. There's a sentence of Marx's writings that says more than a lot of long speeches. It goes something like this. "Philosophers have long tried to understand the world. We're trying to change the world." How much harm that divorce between soul and body has done! Here, this book on the table, *The Alternative Future*, by Roger Garaudy, has something in it I'd like to read to you:

Today's youth find religion more difficult than ever to take seriously because consistently for a thousand years the churches in the West have taught the worst kind of escapism and have furnished "spiritual" justification for every kind of dualism: body-soul, class, political power [New York, Simon and Schuster, 1974, p. 23].

When Garaudy talks about dualisms he's talking about a great many things, all flowing from the soul-body dichotomy.

When we speak of "servile work"—slave labor—suggesting that some other kind of work—that of free persons, "liberal" work—is somehow superior, that's sheer blasphemy, on the lips of someone claiming to follow the gospel. And with the help of the catechism we've been blaspheming for centuries now. In the gospel this division in human nature simply doesn't exist. The human being is simply "earth" or matter that thinks, loves, and prays.

You recall, Pedro, that when we were talking about the Eucharist we saw that persons "build communion" in church on the emotional level, the intentional level, the "spiritual" level—in other words, on an idealistic level. They don't build it on the level of labor and distribution of goods, the level where matter comes into play, the level of a person's everyday doings, the level of concrete history. This soul-body separation, and our whole idealistic heritage, makes it possible for Christians to *speak* of "communion and fellowship, peace and justice" with perfect clarity, while neither making peace nor building communion nor doing justice.

During my "Roman days" there was a communist who accused Pope Pius XII of having done more for discord than for peace. And he told him so, in violent words. Perhaps he was mistaken. At any rate he had no right to point the accusing finger at one person. After all, what do any of us know about when and how we cooperate with peace or discord? But what I thought was horrible was the way the pope was defended. A scholar defended the pope in a conference. He had all the pope's addresses, all the "diplomatic documents," all the proofs that Pius XII had "done so much for peace." This is the fruit of idealism. No accusations had been made against speeches. They had been made against the Vatican's existential position, its decisions, its money, its investments. The defense completely missed the point.

"Utopia" is different. Utopia is believing that something that is not occurring now can come tomorrow: that persons could treat one another as good neighbors, that men and women could agree with one another, that the human couple could form communion. This can happen, and it must happen. We must see to it that it happens. Idealism makes you content to live in an imaginary world, hems you into a present that doesn't exist. You believe in it because it's in your head. Utopia torments you. It calls on you to go in quest of something that doesn't exist in the present—something you have to "get to." Medical researchers will not rest until they've eliminated disease from the world. They never will eliminate it. But they struggle desperately toward that goal. And the power of their hope is what Saint Paul defines as "hoping against hope" (Rom. 4:18).

The gospel champions utopianism, not idealism. The gospel doesn't hold itself out as a scientific theory. We have to put it into practice, and in implementing it we understand it gradually more and more. The problem is that we regard the gospel as a philosophical theory, and try to develop it, extend it, enrich it, like any other theory. Then it dies. What we take for the gospel is really Christian ideology.

Now we're in a position to understand why Jesus was so little concerned to expand the frontiers of his activity beyond his small group of followers. He preferred to stay with them, and "build communion" with them, telling them about his Father:

> As to you, avoid the title "Rabbi." One among you is your teacher, the rest are learners. Do not call anyone on earth your father. Only one is your father, the One in heaven [Matt. 23:8–9].

The Father is seen and understood "from within"—from within a group of sisters and brothers. And Saint Paul, who always seems to be on the road, lived in community for years. His letters witness to it.

Today there are, you might say, two ways of being Christian. One is the people's way. The other is the middle-class way. (I wouldn't want to delineate an "intellectual way," because I know intellectuals who are more in agreement with the people's way than with the middle-class way.) The people's way of being Christian is to read the gospel right from where a person is in life, and understand it in life. The more you eliminate self-interest from life, and concentrate exclusively on "building communion," the better you understand the gospel. The middle-class way is the speculative way—the way that ascribes more importance to reasoning, to the persuasive nature of certain ideas, than it does to life.

In earlier times zealots would fight to the death over a dogma—for instance, whether Mary was a virgin after the birth of Jesus or whether she lost her virginity in the process of giving birth. Today we fight in a different way, and for different motives, but the battle goes on. Perhaps this is a sign of the vitality of our faith.

Today the struggle is between "speculative" Christians and "practical" Christians. (I might call the latter "historical" Christians if they wouldn't be offended.) Speculative Christians accuse practical Christians of paying too little heed to "truth." They say the gospel is primarily truth, and that you can't act without a clear idea of the truth. Frequently they confuse "truth" with clear ideas.

You pointed out a good example yourself, Pedro, after we read the bishops' pastoral letter on the family. "That's not the Venezuelan family!" you exclaimed. And the people's reaction to the documents of the church has seemed to me to be the one that is more "true." Of course God is Father, Jesus is God's Son, and when the priest says, "This is my Body," the bread is the body of Christ. But stop right there. Don't reason it to death.

The gospel means this: we go to the Father by building communion among ourselves. Becoming brothers and sisters to one another is a lifetime job. We'll never be able to say, "There, that's it now." This is something that can be understood equally well by a Bojó *campesino* and by the greatest scientist on earth.

Not the Poor, but Ideas about the Poor

The conflict begins in Jesus' time. Jesus is in agreement with the Pharisees that the people of Israel has been chosen by God as a dialogue partner. He respects everything that God has entrusted to the people. He does not touch a "jot or tittle of the law." But, people of God, there is something you have to get straight. Instead of repeating, "Lord, Lord," seek to become children of your Father. Instead of speaking of freedom, seek to become free. Instead of decreeing how children are to behave vis-à-vis their parents, begin to love your father and your mother tenderly.

In order to avoid telling Jesus to his face that they did not agree with him—that would not have gone very well with the people—the Pharisees tried to trip him up on points of doctrine. They led him onto their own ground, so as to be able to say, "This man is a heretic. He blasphemes. He disagrees with tradition."

Well, Pedro, centuries have passed, but things have not changed. Perhaps it's a law of history. Perhaps this is the way things have to be and we have to accept it. If, by some miracle, all the priests, all the doctors of theology, could make this statement: we have no ideology to defend, no body of truth to safeguard, let us all follow Jesus directly and join together in one family, so as to be daughters and sons of the Father—the gospel would be truly, visibly, the great leaven of history, and humanity's salvation. But this is only a beautiful dream. I wonder if it would even be a good thing.

At any rate, this is why Jesus had to go looking for "outsiders" to understand him: the Samaritan at the well, Zacchaeus, the Canaanite mother, the centurion—persons who had nothing to lose, and who discovered within themselves an absolute trust in Jesus. "We'll do whatever he tells us," was their attitude.

It's trust that counts. I can know who Jesus is and not trust him. But, to finish this line of reasoning—I can see you're getting bored, Pedro—let me tell you this. There's an idea in the New Testament that has always made a profound impression on me. It's the one about "professing truth in love" (Eph. 4:15). Truth is believed by being done, and is done by being believed. The Greek philosophy that once upon a time intertwined with the gospel has a basic flaw. It's idealistic. It goes straight out of the head and into life. You sit and think, you work out a plan. And then you see whether you can use your plan in life. If you can, you're on top of the world, because the clarity of your plan gives you a great satisfaction. But the gospel tells us: seek truth in life.

Pedro, you've heard so much talk about "popular religiousness" in Latin America. Even this has to be a bone of contention! No one ever goes to the heart of the problem, no one ever approaches it concretely. Should the saints' statues stay, or should they be thrown out? You've heard conversations in our house that really "got to" you. After all, you're a scion of the people. And you've told me more than once: the way some priests treat the people is outrageous. For instance, why should the doctor's wife and the schoolteacher be invited to the Bible-study group on Tuesday and the maid to the Stations of the Cross on Friday? Would you mind, Pedro, if I recorded your comment? "That stinks!" When "popular religiousness" is regarded from without, *of course* the people

will be outraged! Popular religion is "dealt with" in pastoral
training centers. And that is not right! Only priests who live lives of
involvement with the masses, sharing their lives, their struggles,
their hopes, can discover, together with them, the essentials of the
gospel message.

The church knows this instinctively. The Vatican II Constitution
Gaudium et Spes reflects the church's intuition. That is, the leaders
of the church are to make the hopes, the sufferings, the real-life
struggles of human beings their own. But that confounded idealism! It will always betray us. Here is the heinous deceit: we think
we're immersed in the popular milieu just by studying statistics and
sociological studies in libraries.

It is utterly false to say that when unlettered persons look at their
way of being Christians simply, and from a standpoint of real life—
that is, in the case of "historical Christians," Christians *in* history,
the real history of everyday life—they're indifferent to "truth."
They refuse to accept abstract truth, that's all. They do accept a
truth that lights up their life. Jesus called God our Father. Everybody understands that. But whether God created the best possible
world, whether God could have created it or then again not created
it, whether God could have created it differently, whether God
changes only exteriorly or also interiorly—are you really interested
in that, Pedro? What you're interested in is enjoying God's self-
revelation in our lives as our Father.

Remember our friend from Montevideo, the atheist who discovered in prison that God was his Father, and after that nobody, not
even the butchers of Uruguay, could really hurt him? He knew he'd
never be left in the lurch—that his imprisonment would serve the
cause of freedom. He'd learned that when you find you're loved by
your Father, you can be much happier than your mournful persecu-
tors. This is reflection on God. This is knowledge of God. It is
knowledge of God from life, not from a classroom desk.

At the Ibero-American University in Mexico City, I said: "The
poor don't get in here. Only ideas about the poor." And we can
nearly always say this where Christians gather. It took me a long
time, but I finally learned why it was that, in the past, the church
had put up so much resistance to Bible reading. The Bible was for
all practical purposes a forbidden book. My grandfather, a "super-
Catholic," had never read the gospels. The reason is: the gospel

leads you to life, and you can read it only from life. The tremendous nakedness of the gospel passes judgment on all Christian treatises, on the whole Christian construct. It judges our conception of the family, our political ideas, all the impossible combinations we have managed to weave.

Idealism shows its influence on something we have reflected on before, Pedro, when you went with me to visit a religious community. You had a problem. You, scion of the people, felt ill at ease. You had been well received, you admitted that. In fact they made a big to-do over you. But you'd thought we were on our way to pay a visit to "Nazareth," and all of a sudden you found yourself in the midst of the bourgeois world. You weren't your usual cordial self, and I felt ill at ease myself. But then I thought: the "out of place" one is me! I've gotten used to swallowing these horse-pills. I've seen, in Mexico and Argentina—not to mention the monasteries of Europe—"houses of prayer" of a luxury beyond that of a good many families of bourgeois society. This year I was in a Benedictine monastery where they were planning an enormously expensive swimming pool. I came to this conclusion: either the monks were all crazy or I had a conception of religious and monastic life very different from theirs. I set myself to thinking: How did monasteries like this come into being?

As you know, Pedro, there is an institution called the Venezuelan Institute for Scientific Research. There is a library there that really puts me in the way of temptation. And it flashes through my mind that I should have become a researcher. Those who do their scholarly work here have an apartment that I'd call, well, comfortable—not luxurious, but functional. This may be fine, because for intellectual work, work with your head, certain conveniences are helpful. I've visited the institute a number of times. Some of the members are my friends. The atmosphere is very pleasant, and doesn't annoy me. On the contrary.

But monasteries seem to follow the same rule! Create comforts for studious persons, for scholars, so they can "produce." Prayer is not seen as an experience of God under the guidance of Jesus and the influence his Spirit. It is an intellectual activity. It's research, it's scholarship. And so there must be comfort and beauty, harmony and music—whatever will foster intellectual activity.

To me this is irrefutable proof of the influence of Greek culture.

The vision of the human being that has come down to us from that culture has had an influence on the Christian faith. The monks in some monasteries must think of the experience of God as a discovery like the discovery of a law of chemistry or astronomy, or like isolating a mysterious, deadly virus. This is the only possible explanation for all this luxury and comfort. The day these monks read the gospel and find that the experience of God is not the product of a perfecting of the intelligence—that it is different from isolating a virus—they'll realize that they've been up against a brick wall all this time. They had been looking for a house of prayer, and all they found was a sterile "research institute."

When God Becomes Present

What is the experience of God? We'll come back to that, Pedro. Just now I'm too upset. If they keep building this kind of religious house today, it will be proof that the Spirit has made us mad. It may be that in an age when the church held the monopoly in education, structures of this sort were understandable. Today they're under the inexorable condemnation of history. They are of temporary use today for housing bourgeois persons who are in a state of crisis. Tomorrow they will serve as meeting places. Let us hope that one day even these meeting places will disappear. Just now they are busy producing "Christian material," and in so doing they are postponing the reading of the gospel.

Seeing that the "true" human being—as we have said—the one really worthy of the name of human, is the "intellectual," this human being merits surroundings of dignity and circumstance. This sort of person is an aristocrat, and should live as an aristocrat. With these citadels for the "prayer experts"—those who practice the human being's noblest activity, who go in quest of life's supreme values—a Greek mentality prevails. Monasteries are replicas of the academies, the schools of philosophy—high-level scholarly institutes.

They are *altogether dissimilar* from the framework in which Jesus and the apostles lived, and where the "little ones" and the "poor" live, to whom the Father is revealed, whereas the wise and the great ones of the world remain in their blindness. It is not just a matter of poverty; it is a matter of a conception of the human being, of God, of the mission of Jesus in the world, and of the type of relationship Jesus proposes between human beings and God. In other words we have to decide whether houses of contemplation are houses of the quest for the God of Jacob or the god of Aristotle. If this is the sort of place where Jesus' activity in the world is to become present and visible, I prefer a den of thieves.

Another difficulty emerges from idealism: its fashion of regarding the earth, toil, things, the body—whatever is not "idea"—as inferior. To look at a flower, to smell it, was considered an imperfection, and this notion has not altogether passed. It is the spirit, the invisible, that counts. What we can see and touch is of no importance. But Jesus has issued us an invitation: Look at the flowers of the field! Yes, look at the lilies! Do you not see how lovely they are? The eternal beauty of God becomes successively present in the things that pass. As the blossom passes through its moment of splendor, God is present in it. Looking at nature is a way of looking at God. At the moment when the poor person is knocking at the door, this poor one is precisely the vehicle of the Absolute for me. They are not two, this poor persons at the door and the Absolute in the sky, or the loveliness of the flower and the beauty of God. The Absolute is identified with the one whose name today, Monday, is Carlos, and tomorrow, Tuesday, will be Francesca, and Wednesday, José.

This is so difficult for us to accept. God is one thing and human beings are something else. And service to God is one thing and service to human beings another? No, Jesus has made these two things one! But between us and the gospel stands a philosophical education that hinders us from absorbing this vigorous, dynamic oneness. God is the permanent one, surely, who abides forever, whereas the human being passes away. But in this human being who passes away and changes is God who abides, just as within the bloom that withers is the creator God, the everlasting source of life.

You, Pedro, have the good fortune not to have had to live through all these problems. You have not had to live in a church in which Christ is present but which makes itself a stranger to him. You pass a great deal of time gazing at these hills around us, and the red evening sky. You've taught me to look out on Andean sunsets, and you've explained to me that this is your way of looking at God, and speaking with God. You know perfectly well that all this is not God, but the window at which God appears.

You, Pedro, know nothing of "matter," "spirit," and "idealism." How beautiful! Now that you've been here, learning what it is to be a Christian, you're afraid to return to your friends—afraid to go back to that "useless little life," that "carnal life." It's an ugly word, "carnal." I use it because it occurs so frequently in the New Testament. Our life here, our quest for God in toil, in friendship, in our conversations, we call a "spiritual life," or "life according to the spirit." And yet the time we spend in study, in "spiritual activity" is scant, and the time we devote to "bodily activity" is extensive: we work, we eat, we sleep. Your time is more the body's than the spirit's. But your life is not carnal. And I know persons who devote the greater part of their time to intellectual activity, and to the spirit, and who are carnal persons. Everything depends on what we're looking for, what we want. Everything depends on knowing why we are here.

7

Rediscovering Jesus Today

Pedro, you've asked me a number of times to tell you about Jesus. Well, I'd say there are four ways of thinking about Jesus. There is the Jesus of the priests, the Jesus of the revolutionaries, the Jesus of the bourgeois—and Jesus the liberator, who is everyone's and no one's.

The Jesus of the Clergy

The Jesus of the priests is the ghetto Jesus. To be honest, we must admit that a great many priests have come from a ghetto. Originally a ghetto was the section of a city where persecuting Christians confined Jews. A ghetto is a closed place, a threatened place. It is on the defensive, and so it is aggressive. It reminds you of a battle encampment. The Christian ghetto, then, is the place where the words of the gospel are taken to construct a theology of Jesus, or a "christology," as they say.

Jesus is God, as is the Father—and so there's another formidable word now, "consubstantial," meaning "of the same substance." Jesus is God, but he is also a human being. Theories and counter-theories have been created to solve the problem of the union of the divine and human in Jesus. Did he think as we do, suffer as we, love as we? Did he too have to learn, or did he know everything? And so on.

I have to admit that movie directors and writers who satirize Jesus cause me a great deal of pain, like my Mexican friend whom you know, who's writing a novel that will be considered blasphemous. Yes, and all those towering, pompous dissertations on Jesus get on my nerves. Abstract tomes wrap you up in a net so thick that you think there's no making a mistake, no chance of a misstep. If you do get off the track, you get hit on the head: you're "no longer a Christian." (The same thing happens in Marxism, and in any political party founded by a "god.") Sometimes this writing about Jesus is inspired by the great love he radiates. He certainly is most attractive! But sometimes, often, these dissertations serve as ghetto barricades. Those inside say: we know who Jesus is. If you want to find out, come in here. But to get in, you have to know the password.

Now, if you've been following my train of thought, Pedro, you know that we've discovered more than once in our conversations that everyone must find Jesus or be lost. No one, absolutely no one, can say at the end of his or her life: "Jesus? Never met him." Everyone, before death, will be able to say: "Why, Jesus, you were right under there—I never would have thought it!" Priests don't get to many persons, in fact to very few in the world. And these few aren't the ones to have understood Jesus best.

You see, Pedro, it's one thing to know who Jesus is—how his intellect works, what his way of loving is, how he could suffer and die—and something else again to understand him. Many know him and don't understand him. And many understand him and don't know him. This is nothing to be surprised at. The same thing happens to us. It's a law of human nature. You've seen letters from persons who don't know me and never will, but who have read things I've written, and some of these letters show that the writer has understood me from head to foot. And it happens that certain persons who know everything about me—where I was born and when, and into what family, whether I'm sick or well—absolutely don't understand me at all.

You can know who Jesus is and not understand him, and you can understand him without knowing who he is. This should lead us to a conclusion: we ought not to go around bragging that we have a "franchise" on Jesus. But to arrive at this conclusion we have to have come a long way. Jesus was not reached by the Pharisees of his time.

The Jesus of the Bourgeois

Then there is the Jesus of the bourgeois. Obviously, Pedro, when I say "the Jesus of the bourgeois" I mean the bourgeois way of looking at Jesus. This is the "private" Jesus—the one at your disposal.

Do you know who the bourgeois are? The ones who don't stand in line. The ones who make an appointment with the dentist, the lawyer, or the psychologist for a certain time. They can pay, so they have the services of the professional, the worker, or any service, whenever and however they wish. You, Pedro, can get a passport, if you're lucky, in a week. But if you're somebody with the prestige of power and money, it'll be ready in an hour.

The experience of these persons leads them to certain convictions, which then become part of their life, their way of looking at life: "I can have everybody at my disposal. There are no insuperable obstacles to anything in the world, and I have the means for everything. I see no reason why obstacles, or anything negative, should arise in my life. After all, I have an almost unlimited power. My relationship with Christ is no exception."

Christ does not have the bourgeois at his service; they have him at their service. Of course, to have him at my service, I have to pay. I have to pay money, adulation, and flattery. For Christ to be happy with me, I have to say that he is my peace of soul, my joy and gladness, my fellowship, that he is a miracle, that he is my everything.

All these words that seem to refer to Jesus really refer to a legendary personage, a character in a myth or fairy tale. This bourgeois view gives the appearance of respecting the divinity of Christ, but when we look more closely we see that it actually relegates him to a sphere that is several removes from the world of human beings, so that the majority of Christians do not know that Jesus was concerned with liberation, equality among persons, justice, or anything else of major importance for your daily life.

Who is Jesus for me? What have I found in my encounter with him, and who is he for me? One day four boys came to see me. They recounted their life experiences. One was a drug addict, one was a Don Juan, another visited brothels, and the fourth—in him I found Jesus. "All these things I have observed from my youth. . . ." Now that I've found Jesus, I must try to understand him.

Do you remember, Pedro, when we were reading Paulo Freire and we stopped to reflect on "education, banking-style"? You deposit physics, math, chemistry, and so on, in your "bank." You grow wealthier and wealthier. Then you are powerful. Now you are able to dominate others. You grow, and this education, centered on your ego, makes you stronger and stronger, ever more secure, with fewer and fewer guilt complexes when it comes to being above others and controlling them.

The movements and groups laying claim to Jesus have become very complicated. There are differences among them, but their bourgeois inspiration sticks out like a sore thumb: their Jesus is the "banker's Jesus"—the "Jesus for me" (even if we are many, marching hand in hand). Here is the Jesus who changes your insides but leaves you indifferent to historical reality.

I want to read you a passage from the First Letter to the Corinthians, chapter four. The citizens of Corinth are the bourgeois of their time, you might say. They like to have fun and enjoy life. They are very "trendy," all up to date, provided they don't have to get very much involved. The new religion preached by Paul is one of the stimulating novelties that is spicing up their lives. They fit Paul's message to a lifestyle of "keeping up with the world," a lifestyle of beauty and intellectual variety, so that Paul's message will look attractive, so that it will be the "latest thing." Among them are individuals who really try to live worthwhile lives. This is why Paul's two letters to the Corinthians are a composite of reproof, sarcasm, passionate counsel—and brimming hope. The famous hymn to love that we've read together more than once, Pedro, is written to the Corinthians. But let's read this one passage together now:

> At the moment you are completely satisfied. You have grown rich! You have launched upon your reign with no help from us. Would that you had really begun to reign, that we might be reigning with you!
>
> As I see it, God has put us apostles at the end of the line, like men doomed to die in the arena. We have become a spectacle to the universe, to angels and men alike [1 Cor. 4: 8-9].

The human being, the young person, has the right to sing, to be glad. Life is a joy in itself. I believe in the song of those who have found Christ, and in him the meaning of life, for I am convinced that only Christ gives us the definitive, overall meaning of life. But a "joy" manufactured in Christian assemblies—that I don't believe in. That's "banker's gladness," closed into the restricted circle of the assembly, and springing from oblivion of the problem of the world.

I remember when I was working only with youth, trying as best I could to give youth an awareness of what it was to be Christian, and of the responsibilities that went with this awareness, and a very important personage of the church told me: "the young don't need to hear about certain problems. They should sing, be happy, live carefree lives, not know about the problems of the world." The trouble is, these young persons get to be thirty or forty and they're still getting together to sing, to be happy, to live a moment of "paradise"—and they forget the drama of the world. I'd rather take LSD than have to spend time with assemblies like that.

The Jesus of Revolutionaries

Then there's the Jesus of revolutionaries. A group of Christians committed to liberation see in Jesus their inspirer, and from certain things Jesus did, and the penetrating, incisive things he said, draw material that will support and foster their revolutionary theories. This has given rise to a dispute that has not yet been resolved. Does the gospel mean that we should be revolutionaries, and actually have a revolution? Many of these Christians—we may as well admit it—no longer believe in Jesus as the co-equal Son of God. They see him as an important, courageous individual who declared war on the system of his time. They see in him someone who has had the courage to say to the mighty, "I disagree with you!" and who died for saying it.

It is shameful, as I see it, that here in Latin America Christ is used as the witness and guarantor of one's own personal radical ideas. "Look, the masses are Christian. We can turn our own ideas into dogma by saying they're 'what Christ wanted.' " This utilization of Christ, I have to say, Pedro, is repugnant to me, even though, as you know, I think Christ's message is to build communion, and this can mean you go to extremes.

I'm not saying all the radicals are like this. I've known some of the committed ones who are admirable, whether they're believers or not, persons of the utmost honesty. I must say, Pedro, here in Latin America, the persons the most open to love, the most generous, the most pure, that I've found, I've found among members of revolutionary organizations. This isn't theory, this is practice.

Jesus is invisible. They don't run into him on the street. And yet he is so present in history, so at the center of the liberation activity of human beings, that everyone must settle accounts with him, must choose, and be either for him or against him.

When I speak of honesty and dishonesty I'm referring to this (I want to be clear)—an individual committed to liberation recognizes in the gospel a message of communion and justice, and in Christ someone who has preached and lived this message. Some have told me they don't know if Christ is God or not, but they know that no one has had an impact on history like his. This is what I call honesty. But if someone believes that Christianity is totally false, that Christ is an imposter, and has to put on a false "Christian" front in order to "get into your house," so to speak—that I find repulsive, and I can't have any respect for an individual of that kind.

We can decide to be friends with Jesus, seeing that he's so likable, and that he has everything we were looking for. But what about *him?* Will he accept *my friendship?* Friendship is a two-way street. How does he regard me? If I had know you thirty years ago, I'd have said, "Go to confession, little Pedro." And then, "Now you're Jesus' friend. Stay that way." Well, I'm not ruling this out. You do come to friendship by criticizing within yourself what stands in the way of friendship, and asking forgiveness for whatever you've done against this friendship. Because you see, Pedro, when we meet Jesus he's already been our friend, he's already offered us his friendship, and so this "new" offer of friendship always has the flavor of reconciliation. But the priest of thirty years ago may have had a rather limited notion, to have thought that continuing to be Jesus' friend meant "not returning to your sin."

Today I'd say that the important thing is to share in Christ's ideal, which can be summed up in one phrase: to build communion by taking cognizance of uncommunion." This is crucial, and I want to stress it with you: Christ's ideal is to *make communion where there is uncommunion.*

In every age, in East and West alike, there have always been preachers who extolled community. It's no great discovery that this is the supreme, genuine aspiration of human beings. This is what we're born for. If you're looking for a book on friendship, on how to make friends, on how to get along with others, I'll get you a hundred.

Jesus pitched his tent in a world of sin. He's not a philosopher or a theoretician or a psychologist of friendship. He is a redeemer, a liberator, a savior. His is not a theory of friendship, his is—to use a word that has gained common currency recently—a "praxis." Otherwise there's no way to explain his relentless preaching, his anguish, his death on the cross. He did not come to sing the praises of friendship. He came to transform enmity and division into love.

This is why the gospel has no ties to certain ways—humanly altogether deserving of respect, surely—of seeking or celebrating friendship. I'm thinking of the famous book by Dale Carnegie, *How to Win Friends and Influence People.* Without an awareness of division, of the sin of hatred, of inequality among persons—without starting here—none of the friendship theories "get into" the gospel. The gospel goes in search of communion in and from uncommunion. North Americans are incurable optimists. In so many of their books and movements, friendship is a tactic, a way of behaving, a form of education: how to become friends, how to like one another. North Americans will pour any amount of money into any "Jesus thing" that gets this result!

Jesus' message is different. Jesus tells us how to make friends—brothers and sisters— of those who hate us, how to go from hatred to love, from uncommunion to communion. This is the meaning of Jesus' life. Those who seek to *build* communion, then—even if we disagree with their methods—are certainly closer to Jesus than those who *presuppose* communion, singing its paeans with guitar and harp and dance. The church has lodged, welcomed, encouraged, and fostered a bourgeois optimism that is an enemy to the cross.

All the so-called orthodox writers on Jesus define him as the perfect, most complete human being. This he is, of course. They attribute to him all *our* good qualities: intelligence, wisdom, good psychology, good health, and so on. But I've just finished reading a life of Jesus by a Brazilian theologian I greatly admire. It's called *Jesus Christ Liberator,* by Leonardo Boff (Engl. trans., Maryknoll, N.Y., Orbis Books, 1978). He says something new about Jesus. He says that Jesus' greatness consists in being empty. He doesn't mean this in the negative sense, in the sense of someone who "didn't have anything," "didn't have it." He means that Jesus has a capacity for receiving as has no one else. Receiving what? Love, truth. The perfect human being is the one who has, within, this one thing: emptiness. He's not a museum, not a department store "with everything."

You see, Pedro, if we could see the primeval blueprint of the world and how it was to evolve, the idea with which the astonishing variety of the things around us began, everything would be simple as simple can be. We shatter truth to smithereens because we're poor. To know a great many things, when you come right down to it, is the sign of a great spiritual poverty. Those who study a great deal, and study well, the further they advance the simpler they become, and simple to an extreme. They become ever wiser, and know ever fewer things. They progress toward an interior simplification. It's like love. You start with a torrent of words—so much explanation is needed—and you end with a glance.

Jesus is simple as simple can be. He sees the world and human beings in a single glance, taking in all that can be known of the world and of men and women. Our own knowledge of these things is extremely partial, and so takes different routes and consists of a knowledge of various points. What artists, philosophers, scientists, and other scholars ultimately seek is to embrace all things in a single vision, and thus arrive at a synthesis of the whole.

One evening, Pedro, we were talking about philosophy. I told you that the philosophy we know starts out with a prime element of the world and goes looking for something—some simple thing—that would explain all the complexity of the world. This has been the goal of human striving since time immemorial. All philosophers feel that what seems to be a diversity, as if composed of multitudinous things, must have originated from one source, as great rivers begin with a trickle of water. How unlikely it seems that there could be one little spring at the ultimate source of the Paraná, the Orinoco, or the Amazon! Now, imagine a trickle of water that would be the beginning of all of the rivers of the earth. Move upstream along any of these rivers far enough, and you'll find that trickle of water.

The Demands of Commitment

We know that the principle of all things, the beginning of all, is love, and that God is love.

The word "love," Pedro, says so much, and says nothing. It must be used carefully. We have so distorted it. It's distorted by being confused with eroticism, and it's distorted when it's confused with the *idea* of love. I think this second distortion is actually worse than the first. After all, eroticism does contain a tiny drop of love. But in the idea of love there is nothing—just words, words, words.

Jesus did not come to say many things. He came to say one thing only: "Love one another." Become brothers and sisters, true daughters and sons of your Father. The more you are committed to the building of communion, the more you will feel and see your Father. The further you withdraw from the building of communion, the more the Father fades, soars, and disappears in the clouds.

Thinkers, artists, politicians, and directors of stage and screen today agree that Christians are vulnerable on this point. You are abstract, they say, your head is in the clouds; you do not serve history. And we defend ourselves tooth and nail, insisting that the kingdom of God is "not of this world," that Jesus was not a revolutionary, and that religion is not political. And the battle goes on.

If we didn't have the gospel, Pedro, surely we'd all go mad. We'd be schizophrenic. The Catholic world is full of contradictory directives. It seems a supremely rational, ordered world, but when you live in it you can't escape the confusion. One day they tell you to enter into history. Christ is with human beings, he shares their hopes, their sorrows, their struggles, their joys! So you plunge right in. The next day they tell you: Be careful. Don't get get mixed up in that strike. Don't join those who want to change the world. One day they'll tell you: Sure, if communists are supporting a just cause, join right in. But the next day they tell you: stay away from them, they'll gobble you up in their big jaws! One day it's "Let us go forth to meet the world! Yes, there are ambiguities there, but the world does seek the truth. Let us accept the world, let us allow it the freedom to search." And the next day it's "You see, it's the press that's pulled the world to the left." Come, now, will you tell me what I'm supposed to do?

Jesus says: Build communion. Don't say you're sisters and brothers. You aren't. The "incommensurable weakness" of the Catholic world—the ineffectiveness of a group so great in number and so poor in means—is the outcome of these contradictory directives, willing and not willing, choosing and not choosing, going only so far and then turning back. It is not the outcome of our mental or psychological makeup, I'm convinced. It's from a lack of incarnation. Become brothers and sisters, the gospel tells us on every page. Of course you'll get your hands dirty. To begin with, you're not clean yourselves, and no means are available to give you absolute security. Only Jesus can say he gave his life as a gift of friendship and friendship alone. Only Jesus never did anything against friendship. Only he has not contributed to discord. We, in our every step toward love, sow seeds of discord too. You work for friendship and against friendship. But don't despair; do what you can, as you can. Only, get involved. And when evening comes—when you withdraw to your tent, before you take off your work clothes, say: "Very well, my hands are dirty. But I haven't gotten them dirty by looking out for myself. I wasn't seeking my own interests, I wasn't concerned for perfection or even a good reputation. I threw myself into that business out there. I took that initiative because I know that what is wanted from me is a contribution to communion in the world. And I see a sign that God is drawing ever nearer to me, and that I am ever more a friend—that I am ever more anxious to build communion in the world."

Pedro, I want to take another look at what we discussed yesterday evening after a visit from some persons who left a negative impression on you. I want to get at clarity by writing down these points. We straightened this out: we are not to judge others, not because of a decree but because we lack the means to pass judgment. We don't know how sick or ill a person is, how free or not free. True, as we grow up, we normally come to trust ourselves more and others less. It would seem that time, and the experience of work, instead of joining us together and opening us up, isolates us from one another. The need for security grows, and with it grows a love of things. The sign that one is drawing ever nearer to Jesus is self-forgetfulness, unconcern for oneself and concern for others.

A famous book that I read when I was a boy, and that I still think did me good, was *The Imitation of Christ.* At one point it talks about two roads leading in opposite directions: nature and grace. Where I no longer agree with the author of that book is in his conclusion, where he says that we must always do what goes against the inclinations of nature. I don't agree. This leads to tremendous emphasis on the will. But it's true that Jesus' activity in us often is seen through aspects of our life that would not be the way they are in the natural order of things.

For example, there's the case I just mentioned: the more you become an adult, and the more an adult becomes a senior citizen, normally—or "naturally," I might say—you become cautious, prudent, mistrustful. You look for security. But the mark of Jesus' friendship is a progressive liberation in the direction of "imprudence," trust in others, a suppleness of spirit—in a nutshell, all the signs of youth.

This "losing ourselves" and being concerned for others has certain consequences. The first is a continual self-questioning—whether our manner of life, of earning money and using it, is selfish or "altruistic." The second consequence is a loyal quest for involvement—any involvement, with all its limitations and blind alleys, that seems to us to contribute more to the removal of obstacles to a communion of brothers and sisters, and to contribute more to forming this kind of communion.

It seems to me that theology should not be so much a matter of ferreting out who God is, as a matter of illuminating contemporary history, without prejudices, in order to help Christians build the reign of God. What means do we have today for building communion? We grasp that an individual belongs to Christ, and is advancing along the path of his friendship, from that individual's ongoing critique of his or her life, and from the overwhelming concern and conviction that he or she can indeed manage to shake off sleep and build communion. If we grow rich, and more and more selfish, mistrustful, closed off to others, then we fail to grow in friendship, even if, through our reading or theological study, we say we "know" Christ more and more.

Religious groups go in the opposite direction from that laid down in the gospel. They start out in a shack and end up in a palace. Like immigrants they recall the hut they once had, full of flies, lacking in every convenience, and they boast that in a few years they now have air conditioning in an apartment with lights in the hallways, a private bath, and all the bourgeois comforts. The gospel goes from riches to "Go, sell what you have, give the proceeds to the poor, and come, follow me." The religious life goes from "Come, follow me," to "You shall have everything, you shall lack nothing; the only condition I lay down is that you ask everything of a superprotective mother who can be harsh in everything else but will give you a materially happy life. You can trust her blindly."

The visit last night left you somewhat embittered, Pedro, because there were some persons here who showed how topsy-turvy things have become in the Catholic Church. The lay person, who was once thought of as essentially depraved, a hellion, a little devil, is now an angel on earth. The lay person has seen, has understood, has gone to confession, is a candidate for canonization, and is now neatly tucked away in the fridge ready to be served up when needed. And the nun, who in the past gloried in the spirit of self-denial, hard work, and sacrifice, now has enough capital to make an oil magnate drool.

Pedro, if you're going to live and work with Catholics, you'll have to have a strong stomach. If you can stand it, you must be strong. I still hope—leave me this remnant of my optimism!—that religious will discover "poverty of spirit," spiritual independence, even though we're willing accomplices, eighty-percent accomplices, of the consumer society and of the most colossal of the betrayals perpetrated on us by our idealistic philosophy. This alone would justify its liquidation. A poor monk in a bourgeois monastery? What a laugh! You throw in your lot with Jesus and his reign—in a daily "business" routine so detailed that it takes up most of your time? Whom do you think you're fooling?

I had a Venetian friend, Pedro, who was from an aristocratic family. He had inherited a palace that had to be abandoned for lack of money. He told me that the entire day's work of one of the maids had consisted in opening the palace windows in the morning and shutting them again in the evening. It's like that in lots of monasteries and religious houses.

Do you know where the reform of religious life is going to come from? From groups of "political" youths, who train themselves by taking up a poor lifestyle, manual labor, a functional diet—just what's necessary—in order to eliminate all their vices and so be prepared for whatever may happen. They consider this training necessary not only to be ready for "war," but to be ready for "power"—seeing that so many politicians, once they come into power, allow themselves to become corrupted by the love of money.

I've been fascinated by my conversations with young persons of this sort, and even more convinced that the Holy Spirit is at work in the world. We've forgotten the existential commitment that Jesus requires of those who aspire to toil for his reign. These young adults seek out an existential situation that is substantially evangelical, in order to prepare themselves for a political mission.

You see, Pedro, Jesus is invisible. That poster in our shack, the one you like so much, is a painting by Giotto, a famous Italian master. It doesn't mean much to me. That is, I like it as a painting, but it doesn't "say" much to me. I've become accustomed to seeing it without seeing it.

One morning last week you told me you felt someone would be paying us a visit. And someone did. How did you have that feeling? We not only have eyes to see and hands to feel, we have other faculties as well, other means. We have the faculty of thought. But we ought not to place too much trust in thought. As we have seen, thought is overbearing: only I know, I alone have knowledge, I alone am judge. It's Mr. Thought who has authorized all the incoherencies that we have seen in our consideration of idealism—and a good many more besides.

How can we come to know Jesus, how we can live in friendship with him? It gives me a great deal of pleasure to speak of this—and at the same time I find it difficult, in fact impossible, not to speak of my own experience. Only a few individuals—the ones called saints—have the right to speak of their own experience. The others annoy me. And I shouldn't like to get on other persons' nerves myself. Jesus is "in style" today. He's on everyone's lips. He's on T-shirts. So we have to be careful not to speak of him in a shallow manner.

8

Jesus: Lover of Human Beings and of the World

I like very much that Cuban song you're always humming, Pedro:

Una historia de un ser de otro mundo,
De un animal de galaxia . . .
Una historia que tiene que ver
Con el curso de la via lactea!

A story of an extraterrestrial being,
Of a galactic creature . . .
A story that has to do with
The course of the Milky Way!

Pedro, you probably think you can imagine Jesus. Long hair and a beard? I've never managed to cook up a picture of him for myself. But he gradually begins to take form out of life itself—right in life. What is he doing inside you? He's told you: leave your house, your surroundings—make a break with that life that means so little to you. And you've felt an irresistible power. You admitted that to me yourself. You no longer enjoy the things you used to enjoy. Your friends have moments of crisis too, just as you. They feel the nausea of life, they get bored. But they stay. They look for a solution in politics, or in some strenuous activity. "But

I realized they didn't really know what it was all about."

And, Pedro, you have said: "Now I feel free from fear. Now I have self-confidence. Now I feel security I'd never felt. I don't know what I'm going to be doing. I don't know my future. But I'm not worried about it. It's as if I knew somebody else were taking care of me and planning out my life. There's no radio here, no tape deck. I have to get up early to go to work. I come back at five o'clock with an aching back. I'm leading a life my friends can't see any sense in at all—and I'm happy. I ask myself, 'Why this happiness?' And the only answer I can find is: I feel somebody's taking an interest in me. I'm interesting to somebody."

We've talked a lot about the word "interesting." It doesn't mean "important." To be interesting doesn't mean feeling important. It doesn't mean a "big deal." You yourself, Pedro, have analyzed it and found it means something like being in love. When you're in love, no one is as "interesting" to you as the person you're in love with. If you're in love, and I ask you whom you want to be with, with whom you like to talk, there's only one answer.

"I don't know why, but when my friends ask me what's new with me, the only answer I can give them is that I feel somebody's interested in me. And gradually, as we read the gospel and talk, I realize that this 'somebody' is Jesus. Something inside me is absolutely sure that Jesus isn't like the rest of us: one day we 'like' somebody and the next day we're not 'interested' any more. I feel he'll always be 'interested' in me. And if I forgot him, he'd come looking for me. I don't know if this is the right way to look at it. I've never read any spiritual books. But I'm sure he'll always be 'interested' in me."

If you ask me who Jesus is for me, I'd answer: Someone who'll always be a great deal interested in me. Someone who'd come looking for me regardless of where I happened to be or what condition I was in.

I dislike writing this. It could look like some sort of "investigation of Jesus." Actually all I'm doing is gathering little bits and pieces from many different conversations, not conversations about "who Jesus is" but about other things, and putting them together.

I do my best not to transmit to Pedro a theology of Jesus, a christology. I may do that later. For the moment, we are two companions walking a path of liberation. I'm trying to break out of my idealism. Pedro is seeking to be delivered, not from vices he doesn't have, but from what paralyzes his "affectivity," his self-confidence—from what he calls his "fear." He has discovered that his friends' disease is basically fear of life. Not a day passes but Pedro doesn't mention to me his concern about his friends.

"What can I do for them? I should give them something out of my experience, but I don't know where to begin. They might laugh in my face. In the little book you gave me on Saint Francis it says that at first his friends made fun of him. They thought he was crazy, talking about 'love and communion.' The same thing could happen to me. I'm a little afraid of going back. I don't feel strong enough. But I feel I ought to pass along my experiences. I could train for politics. I could be a union organizer. But my friends are disappointed with the politics they've run into. None of my friends have known love. They've enjoyed girls. They've 'had women.' But that's all they know about 'love.' They never had any affection from their fathers, any more than I did.

"Until now I've never felt anybody was interested in me. Lots of us have known our mothers' tender love, but we also knew that that wasn't macho and we got rid of feelings like that, but fast! We treat our mothers the way our fathers treat them. Mother's the one who always has to have dinner ready, who has to do the washing and ironing, who never irons our pants right, and who always either doesn't bake the bread long enough or burns it. Not that we actually think about it, but we look for every way we can to be bigger machos, and more and more superior to women. We get it into our heads that women like big, strong, masterful men, men without any gentleness.

"I've never been able to have a serious conversation with my friends. Now I'm making a discovery: Jesus is asking me to put myself at his disposal to build communion. I feel that if I want to feel loved, I have to love. This makes me sad sometimes. It worries me. I feel a great need to do something and I don't know how to do it."

Well, Pedro, I can't give you a little book with ten lessons in it that you can give your friends. I believe Jesus wants this of you, and that he'll see that you discover the way. One thing is sure: you should go back to your neighborhood. Or some neighborhood—it doesn't actually make any difference which. And you should try, along with your neighbors, to build communion. We've said this so many times it's practically come to be an obsession.

I'm sure your concern comes from this: that even for you Christianity means spreading ideas, having a theology to teach. This is really what you're worried about. Any intellectual complications, anything like playing teacher, depresses you. But once you're into the task, I'm sure you'll do a fine job of sharing what you're now living. I can't give you advice, because I'm not trustworthy. I can't shake completely free of Christian ideology, and your job is to transmit the love, the liberation, that you're living.

I can see two ways, two styles, of telling somebody something. One is Saint Francis's. Transfixed by love, he ran about, shouting to each and all that Someone is madly in love with every one of us. The other way is simply by sharing one's life with others in such a way as to help them not to become depersonalized, and help them along the pathways of the actual struggle to become more truly brothers and sisters to one another, more "equal." I don't know which way to tell you to go, you see.

The fire in your insides is Jesus. If you didn't do anything—if you went back to your old life—that fire would go out, little by little. If you make up your mind to forge ahead, that fire will be like a fire in a windstorm: it'll get hotter and hotter, till you're all ablaze. It'll become clearer and clearer what you're to do.

Poverty: Sign of Communication with Jesus

Well, we've discovered that Jesus is someone we can't resist. The other day, Pedro, you exclaimed, "We ought to have another Saint Francis!" Well, who made Saint Francis? Don't you think God could make another one today? Certainly today's Saint Francis wouldn't be the same, but there are three things necessary, urgently necessary, in the world today: *poverty, identification with the people, and a deep conviction that Christ Jesus loves human beings and the world.* These three things—the only things the world needs—can't be taught in the "institutes" of Bogotá, Louvain, Rome, or Madrid. Teachers and students are just wasting their time and money. These things, Pedro, my friend, only Jesus can give you.

Today you told me about the prayer you found: "Fire, burn

me!" I have faith, a great deal of faith, that if persons like Saint
Francis are needed, they will appear. I won't be one. I couldn't be.
But I'll be happy if I can see them and recognize them. If you keep
in mind the three great needs we've spoken of so many times, you'll
have three earmarks by which to recognize "new precursors"
among Christians—the ones you can count on and put your hopes
in. The earmarks are: identification with the people, poverty, and
experience of the great love that envelops the world.

This evening Ramón told us about the two-day renewal retreat.
The priest took his meals alone, in the dining room reserved for
aristocrats. Ramón could tell right away it wasn't going to be a
matter of renewal, renovation. We can't get away from being the
ruling class! And that's why the road to genuine renewal doesn't
pass our way. We can proclaim it, we can desire it, but we can't
accomplish it. It will never be accomplished by those who seek to
renew the world without giving the world the certitude that it is
loved. They may have renewal techniques, but they're ignorant of
the energy, the dynamism of renewal.

A gift of God I prize very highly is the gift of not feeling
necessary—the gift of enjoying seeing others being much more
necessary as architects of the reign of God.

Our conversation about Jesus started when we were looking at a
photo of you, Pedro, in cowboy boots and a hippie T-shirt. "Look
at the little bourgeois!" you said. You could scarcely believe you'd
changed so much in so little time. I can only see you from the
outside. I couldn't tell you you've changed all that radically. And
maybe you haven't really had to. If the only bourgeois thing about
you was the shirt, that's not so bad. The essential thing is not to
ascribe importance to things that used to seem so important. This is
poverty, and I don't mind telling you that it's the poverty proposed
to us in the gospel. I want to talk about it, because you know it's
been talked about a lot in this shack, and heatedly.

For me, poverty is one of the clearest signs of whether you're in
communication with Jesus or not. There's a fellow here in Bojó
who's become everybody's friend, Juancito. He has a big family,
and he's poor, really poor—he's the only one in the village who has
to work for someone else, since he's the only one who hasn't a scrap
of land to call his own. Now, Pedro, do you think Juancito has
"considered the problem of poverty"? Do you think he wonders

"how to be poor"? He wonders how to take care of his family the best he can, how they're not to lack the necessities of life, day after day. When you've encountered Jesus, and entered into communication with him, you get rid of a mountain of concerns—how to dress, how to get a motorcycle, how to buy a record player. Everything is absorbed into one concern and one desire: that famous reign of God, of which we have spoken so often.

When someone has the time and opportunity to get together with others to *discuss* what poverty is and how to live it, I don't see how that person has Jesus. Seen from the outside, as one characteristic of someone's life among so many, poverty is ridiculous. The poor are ashamed to talk about it. I don't know, it's like . . . it's like talking about an epidemic that's ravaging the countryside. I'm a stranger, and I come to treat the sick. I take the risk of catching the disease. But I don't go around talking about the disease, as if it were something good. I don't ask how I can get it, so my eyes will droop and my face grow pale, because this disease will "look good on me."

During the French Revolution, women used to have their hair cut "guillotine style"—all chopped off very unevenly, the way they'd cut women's hair before guillotining them, so there wouldn't be any problem cutting their heads off. They would wear a red ribbon around their necks, to represent their heads cut off from their bodies. I find that incredibly tasteless. Perhaps if I'd seen it in context I wouldn't be so horrified. Somehow, when poverty is spoken of as something in itself, and spoken of with an objectivity that one can either experience or not experience, indifferently, I'm reminded of the choppy hairstyle and red ribbons. You'd think the conversation was about some spectator sport.

Was Jesus poor? "How" was he poor? This sort of question has been asked endlessly. He lived with the poor, but he went out to dinner in Bethany—to an apartment on the east side of Caracas, you might say, or as we would say in Italy, to Parioli. He was poor, but he let someone spray him with French perfume! We religious have spent our time discoursing about poverty because a concern to *build communion* in a world where brothers and sisters are killing one another hasn't so much as occurred to us. To us, proclaiming the reign of God means *explaining ideas* in the clearest possible way. It's easy to see, then, how we can spend years discussing what poverty is.

Involvement with the People

The groups of young persons involved in fighting imperialism, a consumer society, capitalism, exploitation, and so on—when they're sincere, and they often are—would find it ridiculous to hear a group of religious discussing poverty. We religious are so tangled up in ideology that we haven't even noticed the changes happening right under our noses. The grandparents and parents of the new generation fought for an ideology. For them political involvement was involvement in a political program. You could call the political outlook of the 1800s "illuministic." The young today have come to realize that their forebears, retreating into cages of an outdated ideology, let the people down, and thus have been lost in the dust of history. *Today's involvement is no longer commitment to an ideology. It is commitment to the people, to the oppressed.* And so political involvement must begin with "proletarization." It must begin by entering into communion with the people, and from there, from this communion, checking any ideology for validity. The effectiveness of any ideology must be verified on the basis of experience.

From this communion with the people there springs not a doctrine of poverty, but a poor way of life, a progressive simplification of life. Loyalty is not secured by the mere will and intent to act in a way that will be consistent with a teaching. Loyalty is loyalty to the people, to the poor. Unless this is understood, and accepted as a cultural change going much further than what we call a "fashion," it will be impossible to understand youth today, and impossible to understand the renewal of Christian life, which cannot but be a manifestation of youth.

I am well aware that this "gets us into a mess." Revelation surely is from above. How can it be reduced to a praxis? I know. And yet unless we take account of this altogether evident cultural change taking place in the sociopolitical realm—the switch from ideology to the person, from fidelity to a program to fidelity to the people— we shall continue groping about in this "century gap."

If you're faithful to this involvement with the building of communion, Pedro, you can be sure you won't return to the desires of the past. And the youth who dedicate themselves to changing the structures of the society in which we live discover that this change can be effectuated only by the people, only by the oppressed. And yet so many religious continue to devote themselves to the interests of the ruling class.

Another sign of friendship with Jesus, of being in communion with him, is a passion for building communion, and building it concretely, with the people—with the visible victims of human injustice and violence. Communion-building must begin with them, and then, from this point of departure, we shall be able to proclaim communion through the way we live. This is the starting point, the point of origin of the radiation of communion.

Pedro, I hope you never lose this taste that has surely been born in you out of your encounter with Jesus—this taste for a poor life. We have discovered that we need little—less than we could have thought. And there is no sadness in this little, because we have the joy of being welcomed and accepted—the joy of true friendship. We must never forget this, in all the changes that we shall be making in our life.

The joy of this life comes from the discovery that we are here not to exploit or dominate, but to seek to love. Pedro, even when I am no longer here, you must tell all the religious you meet that *poverty* does not exist. Only the *poor* exist. Christ does not will poverty. He wills that we build communion in the world. Communion can be made only by the oppressed class, and from a point of departure among the oppressed, and in order to build it from and with them we must love them, share their life, and *live* a profound communion with them. Then, obviously, Christ will lead you to take positions that others will see as threatening, and you'll find yourself immersed in polemics.

I believe, I intuit, Pedro, that your mission will be not so much one of speaking, but of living. Only youth who discover poverty in this life with the people can restore meaning to a genuine poverty. Now you understand why I find many speeches about "poverty," including some you've heard in this house, repulsive, really repulsive: because the gospel places the accent on love and love for the poor. There is only one, simple way of examining my life and circumstances in order to determine whether I am poor or not. I need only apply the formula: *where the poor do not enter, Christ does not enter.* If our circumstances, by reason of our wealth, or even by reason of our residence in a neighborhood where no poor come—I'm thinking of blacks in South Africa or the United

States—are such that as a matter of fact, regardless of our interior dispositions, a poor person cannot come there, then you can be sure, infallibly sure, that Christ doesn't come there.

At the same time, you'll see that Jesus will give you another sign of his presence. Like a true friend, he'll invite you to "rest a while" with him, to make you feel his friendship, to make you feel that you're his brother, the son of a Father who likes you, really likes you. When you've got a friend, you're not always going to be treating problems of the "ideal." Sometimes you're just going to sit down and rest, and to talk about things seemingly of no importance.

I don't know how to explain it to you, Pedro, but you've mentioned it to me yourself. You've told me that when you've been sitting a long time watching a sunset, you no longer look at it as you did at first. You feel as if you're looking at it with different eyes—as if all these things had been created and put there for you, for you to enjoy. This is feeling God, and feeling love.

You've heard, even from your friends, Pedro (I was right there): "God? There must be somebody, otherwise how do you explain the world? Who's made all these things be?" This is a "cerebral" argument. That is, it's inside the head, and strong as it may seem, it's arguable one way or the other. As far as I'm concerned, it hasn't impressed me much. But what you experience is a completely individual affair. It's like somebody who comes home and sees flowers on the table, finds the table beautifully set, and notices from a number of special things that someone has been waiting, and waiting with an immense desire. Someone likes—really likes—the person expected, and has said so with the language of things. Words wouldn't have said as much. Many don't know how to read this language. Faith, when it becomes deep, is the ability to decipher this language of God who is speaking to us.

If you tell about it to the first person you meet on the street, you won't be understood. It may be that even prayerful persons won't be able to understand you. If you say: God is in the blossom, in the cloud, in the stars—practically everybody will understand you. Or at least they'll think your language is beautiful, full of poetry, like a folk song. But if you say you've noticed that Jesus likes you a lot, because you feel accepted, welcomed, by *things*—few will understand. Very few. I'd advise you to keep your secret, because you could spoil everything. But even if you don't reveal your experience, you'll get it across in other words.

Persons are often strangers in their own homes. They don't feel welcome, they don't feel accepted. When they feel welcome in the world, when they see all creation as a gift, and feel themselves to be at the center of a great adventure in friendship—believe me, Pedro, this is the good news, this is the gospel we must proclaim. This was substantially the message of Saint Francis. I'd even say it's not worth it to build a more just world if it would be an unpleasant world. Imagine if you hated the house you lived in, because it was in a hot, humid, ugly place with no beauty around. Now suppose you could improve your house on the inside, install some conveniences. It would certainly be more pleasant now. But you still wouldn't love your home, and these modifications wouldn't have made any substantial change in your dissatisfaction with your "poor living conditions."

How often I've told you, Pedro, that fellowship is essentially contemplative! This is what I mean by that. Contemplation leads us to want to fight for justice in the world. I hope our conversation has made this idea a little clearer for you.

9

Restoring a Beautiful House in a State of Collapse

We'd begun to talk about the church. You asked me a question, Pedro, that stopped me dead. You asked me whether you belonged to the church, because you'd heard me speak of it with sadness, speak of it critically.

The gospel gives us Jesus' strict orders: judge not, so you won't be judged. You'll be measured by the same measure by which you measure others. We have no right to judge. And we lack the means to make a judgment, as I've mentioned before.

Imagine a woman going to a psychiatrist. The patient will begin to delve into her life. The psychiatrist wants to know about her infancy, whether she was liked or not, then about companions of childhood and adolescence, how she was treated in school, and so on and so forth. The psychiatrist's essential aim is to deliver the poor sufferer, who no longer has a life worthy of the name, from guilt complexes. Then the patient may live in peace.

For Jesus, there's such a thing as sin. There's an objective difference between good and evil. But subjectively—in the concrete case—is this person free and responsible? Could he or she have acted differently or not? What do *I* know about it? Then why should I judge?

At the same time, the gospel calls on me to have a spirit of criticism. It tells me to keep my eyes open. The last page of Saint Matthew, the page we know almost by heart, says that there are the "elect"—those who have known what life's all about and acted accordingly—and the "lost," the failed ones, who will be asking: "Well, when did we see *you*?" In other words, not everyone sees Jesus. His presence isn't translucent. You have to keep your eyes wide open.

We have to build the reign of God in a world full of confusion and contradictions. It can't be done without a spirit of criticism. This has been very unpleasant for me in the church. The young do not have a spirit of sound criticism inculcated in them, and so they easily slip into backbiting. There's an unhealthy, cowardly atmosphere of detraction in church circles. The bishop, the nuns, and every last lay person are its victims. And it's inevitable, because, where criticism is forbidden, you will have backbiting. Backbiting is "criticism gone sour." Detraction hurts. It's life's smog, whereas criticism is oxygen for the brain. Our thought is movement and life, and the life of thought in criticism. I'm not telling you this in my own defense—I'm not a saint; I've fallen into detraction more than once.

Two changes of special importance took place in Catholicism in reaction to the Protestant movement. Doubtless the most important Protestant was Luther. Luther addressed the problem of faith and the problem of the church. As for faith, he said that the important thing was to have trust in Jesus, have trust that Jesus saves you even if you've fallen into the deepest well on the face of the earth. It's not so important to do good, it's not terribly serious to do evil; the important thing is to have trust in Jesus. And as for the church, he said that there's no distinction among bishops, priests, and simple Christians. We're all equal and we're all priests.

The Catholic Church felt under attack, and it stiffened. It radicalized against the Protestant movement. In opposition to Luther's somewhat idealistic and romantic *fiducia*, "trust," the church put a great deal of emphasis on doctrine—on the whole corpus of things we ought to believe—and the person of Jesus was somewhat left out of the picture. This explains why Ramón, who wants his children to make their First Communion, asked us the other day "what you have to know" to make your First Communion. Believing has become practically tantamount to knowing. Little by little faith has become the privilege of those who have an opportunity to study, and the rest are supposed to "believe" on the word of the "leaders." Not since Saint Francis has there been a popular movement in the church. Church movements, instead of being a way of living the gospel, are "apologetical." That is, they arise in defense of the church. This is the service they render. Those wishing to do something for the church must have done studies. What has happened here is analogous to what has happened in capitalist society. Eighty percent of a country's resources go for defense, for weapons, and twenty percent to construct, to create. The priest is a "learned man," the masses say—with respect and distance. In the gospel, the background needed for working for the kingdom is: Come after me. Christian ideology has sprung up instead and "dug in." It is an ideology that withdraws the church from the people, that fails to make the people a church. I'm convinced that many of those who make a public profession of faith—once, twice, or frequently in a lifetime—are without faith in their lives.

The Franciscan movement is the people. There's nothing to "understand." There's only living the gospel. Then where is that "spirit of criticism," you ask? Must one who follows the gospel be ignorant and simple? How can such a one be "critical"? Living in this village, sharing the life of the people, involves a lot of problems. What can be done to help them know one another better, like one another better, not isolate themselves, become familiar with the problems of Venezuelan *campesinos*, take up their struggle? After all, being brothers and sisters and building communion means emerging from one's private cave and taking on the problems of one's brothers and sisters, beginning with those who have the same occupation, and so have related problems and common objectives. This isn't ideology, it's consistency. After all, we've accepted the building of communion as our life program.

This calls for a critical, vigilant, alert spirit. What would Saint Francis do today? I can't tell you, and it may be idle to try to imagine. The important thing is to welcome the spirit, the deep inspiration, of "Franciscanism."

One of the results of so much anti-Protestant insistence on "good works" and "being good" is that Catholics emphasize personal, internalized goodness. They are not much interested in their relationships with others and with history. It's as if their goodness were bottled up within themselves. I can be a good pianist by shutting myself up in my room and practicing nine or ten hours a day, but I can't be good in an evangelical sense unless I'm involved in personal relationships.

I once gave a talk, as I've mentioned, in which I stated that a person is a relationship. Well, they almost wanted to burn me alive! I could see I'd touched on a sore point, as when you say "Ouch!" and the doctor knows where the trouble is. The love you hear talked about here, there, and everywhere in Christian circles isn't generally presented as a relationship. It's an initiative taken by an individual and offered to another individual. Who will liberate Christians from individualism?

This is why we must come right out and say that love is relationship, a basic change in relationship, and that in this change you have everything: the economic, the psychological, and the spiritual. Why is my definition—"the person is a relationship"—so scandalous? Because, in our mentality, the person is a complete being *in se*, the substratum in which a relationship resides. I wanted to skip over all this and get to the heart of the matter. But in our circles this is dangerous.

In order to counter Luther's second position, that we're all equal in the church and that the only priesthood is the priesthood of Christ, the Catholic Church radicalized its notion of hierarchy. Now, I don't deny the distinction between the faithful, the priest, and the bishop, but what happens in practice is painful. Priests and bishops feel themselves to be the only teachers and judges. The laity has no right to judge. I think that it will only be lay persons who have not studied theology who will be able to deliver us, liberate us, from ideology, and help us to reread the gospel.

In a nutshell (I always come back to the same point!), to be a Christian means to build communion, and this communion-building is an obligation incumbent upon all without distinction. Some will do it more technically. Others will do it more intuitively and simply. But basically, this is gospel. We must free ourselves from a certain way of thinking. One does not go from an idea to life, one goes from life to an idea. If you do it backwards, you may get stuck in your ideas, and think that *they* are life.

What Should I Like This Church to Be?

And so, Pedro, to finish our talk on the church: I feel myself to be a Catholic, and I accept the church the way it's structured, and at the same time I don't accept it. You're looking at me a bit strangely.

But if you think of your friends, the young Venezuelan men we know, the ones committed to change, you can get a pretty good idea of what I mean.

Let me ask you two questions. Do they love their country or not? And who love it more, they or the merchants and entrepreneurs who hang out the flag on July 24 and feel themselves very patriotic on condition that no one gets in the way of their business? You answer that your friends are "more Venezuelan" than the others, and that they really begin to be Venezuelans when they get involved in the liberation struggle. They're not trying to destroy Venezuela, wipe out Venezuela. They want it to grow, they want it to shine, they want it to be really important, and so they want to change it. They want its structures to change, its concept of justice, its class relationships—in other words they don't want oppressors and oppressed anymore, persons who suffer so much and persons who are too well off. They want there to be a people of sisters and brothers. Their critique of the Venezuela we have, its present social structure, doesn't seem to you to be motivated by hatred, but by love, by real, genuine interest.

Analogously: Do I love the church or not? I love it as it is, yes, I love it as a sinful, prostitute church, I love it, sinner that I am, because I, too, contribute to its corruption. But I'd like to change it.

How ought the church to be? I don't know. I'll tell you, in one phrase, though, that I'd like it to be a communion of sisters and brothers, a church of the people. I have to tell you, Pedro, never until this year have I felt the problem so acutely. It may be your presence here, it may be my experience in other parts of Latin America. But I don't think I've ever felt so acutely the problem posed by church that is not a church of the people, not a church of the poor. And it ought to be a church of the poor. I'd like the lowly to feel at home, to hear their own language, to discover that Jesus turned first of all to them, and that those who don't belong to the category of the simple must go to the simple to find the revelation of the Father.

I understand that you can't destroy the church and build a new one the way you tear down an old house and build another. You have to stand inside, ready to fight, looking around for what isn't going right, for what holds the poor at a distance. This is the way we'll help change the church without putting an end to it.

We've been on this subject for a long time. And I haven't defined what the church is. That is, I haven't answered your question, Pedro. The Catholic church is a group of persons, a community, who believe in Jesus and are in agreement with what the bishop of Rome and the bishop of the local diocese propose for their belief, and try to live according to the norms of the gospel. It's a group of persons who not only believe in Jesus as the Son of God, master and teacher, guide—but who place themselves at his disposal so that he may make use of them as a group. We are the church. There are leaders in the church, persons responsible for its direction, but they aren't any more important or necessary than the others. Shall we read what Saint Paul says to the Corinthians about this? He says, "God has set up in the church first apostles, second prophets, third teachers. . . . There are different works but the same God who accomplishes all of them in everyone" (1 Cor. 12: 28, 6).

People, bishops, and priests have their particular functions. It's possible that a young person could have more importance, and do more, than a bishop. Once you're a member of the church, you have a creative function in the church. Think of the time of Saint Francis. The church couldn't have gotten along without a pope, and couldn't have gotten along without Saint Francis. Which was more important? I think this is an idle question that would only be a waste of time to try to answer. I'd say: both. I only wanted to tell you that God can use you, then God can give you a very important function, just as God can use anyone else.

I remember an Italian bishop who told a group of young persons that it seemed to him they were too restless. "Take it easy," he said. "We'll watch out for the church. That's our business. Yours is to obey." That's not correct. All the "heads," all the rulers say: "Don't get restless. We'll take care of the country. We're the leaders." But it's a fact that if the "base," the people, weren't restless—if it weren't for the groups who notice that things aren't going right—we'd still be back in the times of the Holy Roman Empire, or maybe even earlier. When these groups, which are minorities, succeed in making the people aware of the need to change, and of the possibility of changing, society moves history and is history. Without this movement at the base, the world would be a stagnant, rotting pond instead of a current of history.

We can't say that things are any different in the church. There are analogies here with political society, as the history of the church shows. The Holy Spirit has moved persons and groups at the base to stir the breath of renewal in the church. This is a matter of historical fact. When I say that it is not the function of the hierarchy to renew the church, I'm not belittling the importance of the hierarchy. The church is a structure both given and to be given, built and to be built, and we all should build it. We all have the responsibility to build it. Again, what we are to build is communion.

You see, in the past the more frequently trodden path was that from church to community. Today it must be from community to church. And for me this is the clearest sign that the church is swept up in a very rapid and profound process of renewal.

Let me explain what I mean. When I was in Rome I worked for a movement called Catholic Action. This organization had its statutes, its purposes, its work. You enlisted in the organization after having gotten a more or less clear picture of what it was all about. My work consisted in guiding groups and encouraging them to stay faithful to the statutes and the hierarchy. These groups still exist, but they no longer demonstrate much vitality. If I had to compare them with other groups, the ones considered revolutionary, I'd have to say, at the risk of oversimplifying a bit, that the Catholic Action groups seem passé to me.

The bourgeois can stand the old structures because they're used to living without hope. They live outside history. You see, Pedro, you and I live out in the open field, exposed to the wind, out in the midst of nature, defenseless, enjoying it and at the same time suffering from it, because we don't have much shelter. The rich can build a replica of this shack, these open fields, right in the middle of town, and have the illusion that this is nature. But it's not. The bourgeois world is used to living with reproductions and replicas of nature. Now that bourgeois structures are in crisis, groups have sprung up that are unconcerned with ideologies, but that strive to live according to the gospel, and attain the objective of the gospel.

What we are witnessing is this: in the past, dynamism flowed from the institution or ideology to the community. Today it flows from the community (not to ideology but) to the church. I hope the institutional church will have the capacity to welcome and to understand these "nuclear churches."

The Church: Built and Abuilding

An institutional church has a need to "irrupt" from without—not against, but from without. Forgive me, Pedro, for not having explained the word "hierarchy" earlier (you see how language betrays me). Basically it means the heads, the leaders, those who give the orders. A function of the hierarchy today should be that of coming forth to meet renewal groups, protest groups, revolutionary groups, welcoming them, helping them to recognize all the distortions, the disloyalty that occurs in all human initiatives—but at the same time, above all, looking for what is positive, looking for what the Holy Spirit is doing in and with these groups. The role of the hierarchy is not an easy one to fill, nor a negligible one. It requires docility, intelligence, patience, and a series of gifts on which I need not dwell longer here.

The church is both built and abuilding. When we enjoy community, we feel united in friendship, and we feel that it is the Lord Jesus in our midst who fashions this friendship. Pedro, this is church. But if we only enjoy it, this same community withers and is blighted, like a plant that bears no fruit. Part of this community's reason for being, yes, is to bask in the warmth of God, like a flower showing all its beauty. But first and foremost this community's reason for being is to reflect on and embrace the struggle for the extension of this communion.

Cultural changes have wrought a change in a certain "conquest mentality" we used to have. I'd like to dwell on this a bit, because for me it's something of the utmost importance. There is so much of my life that it has had a bearing on.

When I began to be a "conscious Christian," the notion of the "militant Catholic" was very much in vogue. Anyone who asked what it meant to be a Christian "for real" was instilled with the idea that a Christian is a conqueror. To be a Christian was to make someone else a Christian—or ten others, or a hundred, a thousand, to multiply them without limit and install them everywhere, in the banks, in politics, in sports. Why? So that whenever the church had the need to defend what it considered to be its rights, in whatever area controversy might arise, it would have its champions, its defenders.

Suppose, for instance, there was question of religious education in the schools, tax-exempt status for churches and church organizations, or some other similar problem. The basic idea, the inspiration behind this approach, was good: Christ is the center of history, the axis of the world, and so there cannot and should not be anything outside him and against him. But the method was not good, because it counted more on influence at the highest levels of government than on the real potential of the people.

As a concrete example, imagine a national hierarchy expressing itself in these terms (in private of course): "Is divorce really necessary? We don't care whether the populace wants it or not, whether it's appropriate or not, or even whether it's just or not. The president can be pressured, so can certain legislators and pressure groups, not to talk about it."

The alternative would be to talk about it with the people, presenting the people with all aspects, showing why and how it goes against the faith, and so on. In other words, you can have confidence in the people. The debate on the question of divorce in Italy certainly contributed to the conscientization of the Italian public. Italians heard opinions for and against, and were able to evaluate both sides of the issue. When, instead, only one bell can be heard in a land, when only one side of an issue is aired—this is not a good thing. When the public is put into a position in which it can reason out and weigh the various aspects, this is good. Working from above, through political influence, and leaving the people out of the picture, convinced that they don't understand, and are not in a position to pass judgment, is certainly not evangelical.

The Christian view that I had at your age, Pedro, was that Christians should be present in all milieus and all walks of life. Christians should be influential everywhere. Christians weren't orientated to building community and to live in community. Quite the contrary, we were trained to conquer, to "make other Christians." A young man was given intellectual training and was trained to be "militant." This is the idea that Catholic Action, secular institutes, and other institutions were founded on: preparing soldiers of Christ on all fronts.

In recent times we have made a great discovery: that it may be that groups that do not know that they are Christian, that do not even wish to be called Christian, or refuse to belong to the church, are actually more Christian than groups inspired and directed by the church. Groups that don't know they're "church" may be more "church" than groups that profess to be.

Why? To return to the same point: because groups that don't know that they're church present the most genuine signs of church. They're united in true communion, they feel the equality of all of their members, and they seek to build communion, often at the risk of their lives. They may lack two elements that are certainly very important: faith in Jesus as their savior—the conviction that there is no building of Christian communion without him—and the acceptance of the church as an institution. But we have to be able to look deeper, and many times we notice that these two elements are *not* lacking.

I think that Christian mission today, rather than being propagandistic, rather than "teaching things," should be that of "explicitating Jesus" in these groups—that of helping them to discover that they're church. And this can't be said from outside. You can't come knocking at their door and say, "Hey, in there, you know you're church? Christ is present in your midst because you want true communion." Only a community that's conscious of being church can help another community make gospel values explicit and discover its actual identity as church. Both conditions must be present: that the community that knows it's church present attractive values, values acceptable to the community striving to build communion outside the church, and that the community that knows it's church be able to discover and admire, in the other community, this implicit, hidden manner of living the gospel.

A new vision like this helps in an in-depth rediscovery of the substance of the gospel, and completely wipes out certain convictions we held in our youth that we thought were Christian values. I don't regret having followed certain ideas in my past, because if you're loyal to Christ he'll help you gradually discover the truth yourself: walking with Christ is walking toward the light. But above all walking with Christ is moving. No wonder, then, that we should have to look over our shoulder and say that we've gotten past certain stretches of the road.

The conclusion is that Christians today don't have to feel like "propagandists," spreaders of Christianity. Rather they are conscious of being genuine members of the church, and of knowing how to put together a community that really and dynamically seeks communion in the world.

A Church Made of the People

You ask me, Pedro, what communion there can be between a community you yourself have seen living in poverty and a bishop who lives in a totally different milieu, who lives with persons who have nothing in common with the members of that community as far as lifestyle is concerned. It's a difficult problem, Pedro, I admit. I've found that in its overall mentality the institutional church is clearly not of the people. It's *for* the people, but not *of* the people. And today that hurts, hurts a lot, because contemporary Christians want less and less to do with those who think *of* them and *for* them instead of *with* them. They feel responsible for their own life and lot. This calls for the urgent renunciation of every form of paternalism.

I've analyzed this difficult problem, Pedro, in this way: I've reflected that normally an essential breach occurs between parents and their children in their respective lifestyles, in their way of looking at life, without any breach of love. Surely they suffer from the fact that they no longer agree on absolutely everything. But I think that this very suffering is a sign of their communion. This is a problem you can't solve in theory. Concrete occasions will tell you whether you're still in the church or outside it. For me the essential thing is to live in the church, and be church. But we must not live in fear, we must not live without courage and daring. We could be looking for the security and tranquility of being in the church and yet be unfaithful to this concrete task of building community. I'm not asking you to make a choice between the two, Pedro. They form a unit. There's no incompatibility between them. But if we're trembling with fear, we'll do nothing.

So, if you ask me whether I want to belong to the Catholic Church, I have no hesitation in telling you yes. If you ask me if I like the church the way it is today, I'll tell you no. Why? Because the institutional church is not the people. And why isn't it the people?

Because its ideology is cut off somehow. It never comes to terms with praxis. Thinking is done for the people, not by and with the people. Consider the liturgy.

What am I going to try to do? Contribute as much as possible to revolutionary changes in the church. I think, with all the sincerity I have in me, that changes can be brought about in society by changing the church, and that changes can be brought about in the church by changing society. They're two aspects of one reality. Being a Christian doesn't consist in practicing a certain private rite; it essentially means believing that a change is coming in the world toward great communion, by means of the concrete actions of human beings, and that Christ comes in as the principal factor in this change, this activity. If the church were a private club, a school of "professionals" in the matter of private prayer, this kind of talk would be absurd. What relationship could there be between change in the church and change in the world? But if it's true that the church is the leaven of history, then by devoting yourself to the transformation of one, you are working for transformation of the other.

And so, you see, Pedro, you have to politicize evangelization and evangelize politics. Don't let the words scare you. I'm only trying to put in a nutshell what we've been seeing and saying. If we toil to build a communion of brothers and sisters in the world, this is political work. But this political work is not total unless Christ transforms the human heart. And so the tasks are simultaneous.

Let me read something to you that Roger Garaudy, a communist, wrote. It will tell you what I mean:

> It will not be enough to suppress private ownership of the means of production, and lodge power with a communist party, to occasion the rise of a socialist democracy, a new person, a new culture, and a new product of civiliza- tion. . . . This faith is not an opium, but a leaven of the transformation of the world. Every organized blow struck at such a faith is a blow against the revolution.

This is why, as I've said so many times, I'm against Christians who say, "First let's have the revolution, and worry about religion later." And I disagree with the other Christians who think that the most basic thing about faith is a relationship with God. I get a pang in my heart when I think of the partiality of the church, which sees danger only when Christians seem to reduce religion to politics, and sees no danger when they try to reduce the gospel to theory and prayer.

Never forget, Pedro, that the three great temptations of the church are idealism, individualism, and dualism. We see the harm these things do when we see how they operate in practice. Idealism in practice prevents the church from being the people. Any support the church gives to movements fostering spiritualism, fostering ideas apart from concrete, real involvement in history, is support for oppressors and oppression. It's help given by the church for the continuation of the world's traumatic divisions, support for the hostility that reigns between oppressor and oppressed. It's an initiative taken against peace and against a communion of sisters and brothers, all mere talk about such peace and communion notwithstanding. All encounters that occasion a realization that we are in fact divided—that there are concrete data and decisions that in fact divide us—are excellent and welcome, from whatever quarter they may come. All declarations to the effect that we are brothers and sisters already, that take no account of the world's divisions—that, as some young persons wrote me, tell us that there is no Third World—are opium.

These conversations with you, Pedro, with our neighbors, show me a new way of reading the gospel. I feel them to be, however modestly, a contribution to a new church, truly a church of the poor. What we can do—you and I, Juancito, Ramón, and María Juana—is to clear the way, open up the way to, this church. You yourself will be able to do a great deal more. You'll still have a long road ahead of you when I come to the end of mine. Yesterday we read that chapter of the Letter to the Hebrews that I like so much, chapter eleven: "All of these died in faith. They did not obtain what had been promised but saw and saluted it from afar" (v. 13). I feel like one of the "these." I see and salute a church that will be more a church of the people, and thereby more of history and in history.

If you read Comblin's theology, you have to cry out once again: for four or five centuries now, the church has not been right one single time in its judgment of great human events—the wars, the revolutions, the political movements. And how dearly it has paid for the privilege of keeping company with the great, the mighty, and the rich. I'd like to see it try making common cause with the poor for once, and see whether things might not go better. And this can't be done by decree. ("Go to the poor!") The only way is for the poor—those who don't understand Christian ideology—to become church.

We always end our discussions of the church on an optimistic note. If the church had been made by us, if it depended on the good will of its leaders or of the majority of Christians—I'd say let's go find something else. But I can't help remembering two things. First, God is building the church. The Holy Spirit is building the church. The greatness of God—we'll see one day that this is true—is better manifested by making use of worn-out, useless tools like ourselves, than if God had done everything alone. A fine church it would be, without human members! It would not be a *church.* And then, I don't know how I know, but I'm absolutely certain the Holy Spirit will manage, in this tangle of contradictions, to build a church of oneness, communion, and love.

The second thing that keeps me from abandoning what I have begun is that the church is the "hypothesis of history." The church is the great, high ideal within the unfolding of history. This is another way of saying that history is headed for the formation of a new humankind capable of community and communion, capable of fellowship, capable of forming a single body, the church we dream of. Perhaps, with so many brains working together, we shall find a new name, on which everyone will agree. For the time being, the ordinary name for this unification of persons and things, the Father's one desire, is: church.

10

No, Prayer Is Not Enough

"No, no, no basta rezar. Hacen falta muchas cosas para conseguir la paz." (No, no, praying is not enough. You need lots of things before you can have peace.")

It's strange, Pedro. I've noticed a change in your repertoire of songs, almost right in step with the lines of reasoning we've taken in our conversation. Your Venezuelan song—Ali Primera's song—is like background music for a subject we've talked about in a number of conversations. Writing about prayer today means running the risk of theory-building, and thus of falling into ideology. Then why have we been talking about it? Because when you told about your experience of prayer that evening in that religious group, you found that you and they were saying different things.

If I told you you were right and the others wrong, I wouldn't be telling you the truth, and I would be placing you in danger of lapsing into hypocrisy. On the other hand, the conclusion you came to isn't right either—"I don't know how to pray and never shall know; I guess prayer's not for me." Perhaps the most correct thing would be to continue to criticize. If you decide to be a Christian, you're not going to be able to avoid the company of Christians, and without a spirit of criticism you can unwittingly slip away from the people by practicing prayer, which ought to be making you more and more part of the people.

In prayer we clearly see the three failings I've referred to so often, perhaps too often. Jesus said something very important, something basic for any reflection on prayer. It's a very, very short

113

passage, and it's in chapter ten of Saint Luke, verses 38 to 42. The episode is very familiar. Two sisters invite Jesus to supper. Martha takes charge of making dinner, and Maria sits with Jesus listening to what he has to say. It's a scene I've witnessed right here in the village of Bojó. When you're invited to someone's house, one person goes to make coffee or something to eat and another, or the others, stay with you. When there's only the mother with her children, the mother tells her children, "Stay here, keep him company while I get coffee ready." But Martha isn't willing to work in the kitchen all by herself. Perhaps she's getting a pretty fancy meal ready. In any case, she calls Maria to come and help her. And Jesus says there needn't be all this fuss, and that Maria's made the right choice for now.

And then do you know what happened, Pedro? This statement by Jesus fell into the hands of persons of the Greek culture that had always maintained that the important persons, the persons who are really persons, who deserve the name of person, are the ones who do not work with their hands, but with their head or mind. And prayer became an intellectual activity, like studying, or reading a book, or giving a lecture in philosophy. Conclusion: class A human beings are those who devote themselves to this exalted activity. So let us all be Marias rather than Marthas! This is the view that, as I've explained to you, Pedro, gave rise to those intellectual monasteries—those houses of study where, of course, some manual labor is performed, but which are nothing like working-class homes, and still less like the huts of country folk. They're very like bourgeois homes, or cultural institutes, museums. But let's not go back over this. The kernel of the gospel episode is: prayer is an encounter with God, a dialogue with God. And so we have to know where God is, where we can find God and by what means, and in what language we can speak to God.

I think that with what we've said, Pedro, you have what it takes to pray. You're sure Jesus is in this world, this world in which you notice that there is more discord than love, and that he's here with the intent of building a communion of sisters and brothers. He's a friend of yours, and a friend you've made not to "chew the fat" with or "fool around," but to change the world—something like that young man who made you a political action proposal. You trust Jesus to change the world, and change it by making it a livable and pleasant world, inasmuch as we've agreed that persons will be well-off and happy in the world when they like one another.

Yes, Pedro, at the risk of being monotonous—I promise you I'll carry to others this message of ours, because we've discovered it in the reality of our common life—any milieu is pleasant where two or three persons gather together, love one another, and communicate with one another on a deep level. Any milieu, even the most comfortable, is unpleasant when persons live together without love. I'll never forget an Argentinian woman who told me how she'd lived with her husband for twenty-five years in an *obraje,* a lumber camp, in the northwest of Argentina. I know this territory, and I knew this woman in comfortable circumstances. I thought her story heroic. "But I had love," she said.

The world is beautiful, but unpleasant, because we don't love one another. Jesus' work is changing it. And it doesn't look as if his work is coming along very well. You've suffered from this yourself, Pedro, because you've seen communities where you expected persons to love one another and understand one another because they were united for the sake of the kingdom—and you saw that this was not the way it was. You picked up remarks that struck you— like, "I can't get along with him." Or, "We don't think the same way. We can't live together." Pedro, you come from a world that's made you feel a sharp desire for friendship, for understanding, and you thought that this would be present in a unique way in a Christian milieu, and you've found that this can be a delusion. Friendship, encounter, is terribly difficult, for everyone. The excuse we can find for certain Christian milieus is that they've had other objectives—pastoral efficiency, intellectual training, unity in doc-trine, coordination in obedience—and haven't aimed at friendship. And Jesus' work is "jammed."

There are many obstacles in us. They're psychological—that is, they come from the structure of our ego, and the history we've lived from infancy onward. Being young, Pedro, you can't see why these obstacles can't be overcome. You still think that with a little good will we could come to like one another. You took it out on *me!* Why don't you try to talk it over with Jesus? Of course, a person could reason this way: "What can Jesus do about it? If persons don't want to. . . ."

You see, Pedro, if you read the Bible, from the first page to the

last, you'll find that the men and women who have felt this problem
and suffered from it, have talked about it with God. We have only
one legitimate complaint when it comes to complaining to God,
only one thing we have to be dissatisfied with: that we don't get
along with one another. You've told me, "Everything would go
fine, we wouldn't lack a thing, we could be happy, if it weren't for
these little 'community problems' bothering us, making us feel
bad."

Well, just transfer that to the world scene. Everything would go
just fine if it weren't for the nuclear bomb and intercontinental
missiles. They're nothing to laugh at, and they keep us awake at
night.

Absolutes, Not to Be Betrayed

All in all, Pedro, you could tell God: "Everthing looks fine.
You've done everything well. The only thing that doesn't work is
the human relationship. I'm not happy with the way love is going."

But what has God to do with that? It's *our* fault. Be straightforward with God. Don't reason too much. If I use my reason and
experience, I come to a conclusion like this: Obviously the reason
Carlito and Francisco don't get along is that Carlito had a domineering father, and now he's projecting his image of his father on
Francisco. Toño doesn't like José because José takes advantage of
him at work. And all these episodes happening before your eyes
compose a great river or lake—this world, where persons don't feel
good because they don't like one another.

We shouldn't say that prayer will fix everything. I'll pray, I'll
close my eyes, I'll open them again, and the world will be paradise,
where everyone likes everyone else. No, the natural, spontaneous,
thing is to protest to Jesus: "What's going on? Why don't you get
busy? Why don't you help us change our mutual relationships?"
The Bible is full of these complaints and protests.

Today, of course, we are much more knowledgeable in psychology, political science, and sociology. We can't dispense with the aids
afforded us by human discovery. Today we no longer ask heaven
for rain. But this search relationship—this human being anxiously
opening up to find another, and through that other still others—
this quest abides. Don't ask God to solve the problem of nonrela-

tionship, Pedro, of discord among human beings, but use prayer to break out of your own shell—to come out of yourself and move toward someone else. Open yourself to that one, and then to still others.

If you read the Bible attentively, you'll notice that human misfortunes are attributed to a forgetfulness of God. Persons have turned away from God, and this has been their undoing. This can be interpreted superficially and coarsely as if God were a great landholder who demanded that human beings continually acknowledge their dependence. Surely there have been persons who have read it this way. But it can also be read as a reproach of human beings for closing up within themselves. They no longer recognize one another as members of one family, brothers and sisters to one another. They've closed themselves up in their selfishness, and this is the cause of all their woes.

How many times have we said that human healing and the salvation of the world will come when human beings break out of their shells and open to others? And we've said that one's neighbor, one's brother or sister, turns out to be an absolute, who cannot be betrayed—who cannot be left in the lurch. Nor will one wish to betray a sister or brother if one understands practically—in practice and not in theory—that for now the absolute resides in this person. And so the encounter with the absolute, with the Father, the human being's openness to the other, cannot be viewed as a kind of magic means of solving the problems of the world that *we* are to solve.

Why should we pray? That's all you ever hear, not only from atheists, but from Christians. We must overthrow the system, with or without violence, we hear. *We* must change relationships, and make them just instead of unjust. The earnestness of the cry is due in part to the guilt complex weighing on Christians. Often—we may as well admit it—we've thought that prayer-as-prayer would fix the world. Today we overreact to our old attitude, and many of us, very many of us, have abandoned prayer as useless. And there is a reaction to this, in turn—a polemical one, which therefore goes to the other extreme—which is (not that of praying too much, but) returning to a revamped notion that prayer "fixes everything."

But I'll tell you two things, Pedro. First of all, don't burn your brains out. Keep it simple. You haven't had a bellyful of prayer in any seminary or religious high school. You've never had the indigestion, and so why join all those who have to "throw up" before they can get over their nausea? Secondly, you can rest assured that we're on the way to a rediscovery of prayer. Let's hope that it will be an evangelically genuine prayer. The road to our new openness to prayer will be the discovery that it isn't true that everything depends on us. True, we have to do a lot more than we thought we had to fifty years ago. We can do more; there are more things that depend on us, not on God, than we used to think there were.

But we discover that there is one little thing that doesn't depend on us. I can tell you this from the experience of two leftists. In practice, they discovered that, when they set about building justice and organizing a new society, there was an imponderable, an unforeseeable, fleeting quantity not subject to human control. Here's something by Alexander Dubček, who was secretary of the Czechoslovak Communist Party. It's from a letter he sent the Czechoslovak parliament:

> We do not live by bread alone. A party bent on being genuinely avant-garde will not be satisfied with pointing to the results of the toil of the people. It must strive for the creative expansion of *all* of society's forces, so that men and women in this regime may be able to project and develop themselves to the fullest—so that they may achieve self-realization.

This excerpt has nothing to do with God and prayer, but it does represent one criticism among many of the notion that once you change economic relationships you'll automatically have a society of brothers and sisters, a society of respect for the human person and for the deepest human aspirations.

The other testimony from the left is a sentence from Garaudy, and it comes pretty much to the same thing. "A purely technical revolution, consisting in a changing of structures, will not enable us to make of all men and women the architects of their own history."

Observations and criticisms of this sort, which are becoming more and more numerous and explicit, ought not to lead us to the conclusion, "Very well, then, it's useless to get involved in trying to change the world." After all that we've said, I don't see how this conclusion can occur to our minds. If it does, let's fight it for all we're worth. It may sound scandalous, but I'll say it again: it's better to work to change the world without praying than to pray without a deep desire to change the world. And the desire must be "efficacious." It must issue in action. If we sit around with our hands folded waiting for the world to change by some kind of mechanical evolution, our prayers will be useless.

But the criticism we've just heard leads me to two conclusions. First, there's something in human nature that "doesn't work." If economic obstacles are removed, we invent some other impediment to our neighbors' being, self-assertion, and growth. In short, a fellowship of brothers and sisters will not arise from without, in virtue of a change in economic and political relationships. Human beings are substantially selfish, or at least historically selfish, as we know them, and do not acknowledge the rights of others, either in word or in deed. And this problem will have to be solved in every type of society, though I recognize that there are societies that are less selfish in themselves, more centered on altruism.

A communion of brothers and sisters comes about gradually. It is the fruit and sign of the "new human being," which, for us Christians, means the reborn human being. We believe that the power to give this life is in the hands of Jesus. This, Pedro, will help you understand certain expressions in the gospel. Jesus defines himself as life. "I am the life," he says (John 14:6). And he says, "Apart from me you can do nothing" (John 15:5). He doesn't mean, "You sit still, I'll take care of everything." He means: "Don't leave me out, don't forget me! Without me you can build a perfect structure, but it will be lifeless. It will lack the main thing—something invisible from without, something not subject to the laws of logic: the mysterious force called life."

The Bible shows women and men immersed in the history of their time from the top of their heads to the soles of their feet, like the prophets—continually risking their lives, hurling accusations against the mighty of the earth, speaking with God at great length, expounding to God the problems of the people, and finding their strength in the fact that they have been sent by God.

Furnishing Hope to the World

The second conclusion to be drawn is that one of the most urgent tasks we Christians have is to supply the world with hope. The effort required for the building of communion in the world is tremendous. The apparent result is paltry. And so men and women are inclined to forget it all and take care of themselves. How many persons you've met, Pedro—and you'll meet even more—who tell you, "When I was young I was a big crusader. Now I realize it wasn't worth it!"

Prayer ought to be the ongoing discovery that God is involved with us and that God is going to stay involved. Here we have the nub of the question of what prayer is. First and foremost it's "renewing the contract."

Today the labor inspector came to Bojó. He found many irregularities. He began by criticizing the workers. He said they don't demand respect, they don't know the laws, they're a bunch of lazy cowards. His face was all red, and we laughed because he got so "het up" he had to take off his jacket although the rest of us were freezing. Will he be saying the same thing to the bosses who do the hiring? I doubt it. I imagine he'll go sit in their parlor with a nice bottle of whiskey and chat. I've told the workers that duties and rights are divided between employers and employees. Employers ought to respect the law, and give employees their due. Employees should honor the contract they have agreed on. You don't need much imagination to guess what this inspector is going to tell the bosses. The laws in Latin America are excellent, Pedro, but they're not observed. And don't think things are much different anywhere else.

The example's not such a good one—it's a poor comparison. But even Jesus used far-fetched examples, as long as they were things his hearers knew about. And they made a great impression. Obviously, praying doesn't mean playing inspector. The example is right on track in one respect, though, because it often happens that those responsible for the building of the reign of God berate the "workers": "You're sinners, you've forgotten God, you behave badly with one another." And they swat you right and left. The preachers I heard in my childhood were famous for hurling thunderbolts at the people. Their successors hurl thunderbolts at the people's "leaders," but they neglect to speak with the most interested party of all, God. It's not out of fear or self-interest, as with the labor inspector—it's because they no longer know which end is up.

The prophets are the ones who, immersed in reality, from within concrete praxis—"from out of political involvement," as our friend Gerardo always says—renew the covenant, renew this pact between people and God. They tell their companions: "Race of vipers, why do you behave so wickedly with your sisters and brothers? Why are you so unjust?" And at the same time they say: "Hold your heads up, don't droop like grass in a drought! Salvation is near!" They are constantly reminding the Father of what he has committed himself to: "Awake, O God! Why do you sleep? Do you not see our enemies crossing all the borders? Would you like us all to die, you who have promised life? How do you expect us to believe in you and trust in you when you let us die this way, like abandoned dogs?" They rebuke, they caress, they sing in every key, so as to persuade their brothers and sisters and God.

Pedro, faith is good for nothing, faith is a bourgeois ideology, if it fails to penetrate life. And it penetrates life when you discover personally that a communion of brothers and sisters, and peace, are the same thing: that both are the historical implementation and actualization of a pact between God and human beings. For prayer to be genuine, the person praying must never emerge from this reality. It is a most serious mistake, with very grave consequences, when Christians, who ought to be totally involved in historical reality, lose sight of this essential mission of theirs to be the intermediaries between human beings and God. It is a grave mistake to leave prayer to those with nothing to do, who fill the void of their fear, their boredom, and their loneliness with a relationship with God invented out of whole cloth, viewing God as someone who is at their disposal. Prophets rise up in a world of tension, at the moment of their people's crying need, such as the moment at which we now live in Latin America today, with their tremendous power of denunciation, with their huge hope, and with their terrible emotionality, as they communicate to the generation of today the everlasting tenderness of God, God's solicitude for women and men. "Even could a mother forget her baby, I cannot forget you."

To get back to our labor inspector. If he's honest, he can't go to employers and talk about something altogether different, or, worse, try to get something out of them for himself. So too with prayer. Prayer can't be genuine unless it begins with a genuine commitment to the building of a communion of brothers and sisters. In other words, if we place ourselves outside this pact, this covenant, this alliance with God and human beings, our prayer cannot be true. Prayer cannot be individualistic—something between myself and God. The only possible dialogue with God revolves around that fantastic contract.

Implicitly you have received an invitation to prayer, Pedro. I can tell you suffer from your incomprehension, the difficulty of this dialogue between us. And the more you speak of this with God, the more you enter into this suffering, and the more you enter into God's secret and find the language of prayer. It makes no difference what you say when your dialogue is the dialogue of a "beginner." You tell me how much it hurts not to know how to build communion. Talk about it with God. I could give you practical advice, but I can't give you the strength that brings persons outside themselves and makes them able to understand God and find God's language.

Prayer will enable you to see ever more clearly, Pedro, how you can make a commitment to peace, and will free you from any impediments to being an instrument of peace—your impatience, your hot temper, your sensuality, anything that can be summed up in terms of self-interest, in terms of being all wrapped up in yourself. Not that a dialogue with Jesus should always be concerned with the problem of peace, of discord in the world, of the "labor problem." As I've said before, there will be moments when you'll just feel glad, feel the repose of being near Jesus. There will be moments when you'll suffer from your awareness of falling so far short of his friendship for you. After all, it's a friendship, with all the vicissitudes of a friendship. Be careful not to let too much "logic" get into your prayer. If you abandon the "affective level," the level of spontaneity, for the level of logic, everything is ruined.

Rather than talking about prayer, let's speak of a relationship. Little by little, you notice, we've gotten into the habit of speaking about Jesus as a third party among us, as someone who has entered this dialogue of ours as an "interlocutor," as we continue to speak, basically—when we're talking seriously—about the problems of the world we live in. The songs you like best these days, Pedro (of course, we've criticized them a bit, too), the newspapers we read and comment on together, the books I read and give you something of the substance of, the observations we make on our everyday experiences—all this is the content, the pith, of prayer.

Christian Prayer

The only logical argument for prayer is that a messenger of God has come among us calling us to cooperate with God in the reconciliation of human beings who are incapable of dialogue. God's presence among us is the contract, the guarantee, that we shall find what we so painfully seek. Jesus' death for his friends, and for friendship, renews the ancient pact.

Prayer removed from this context is no longer Christian prayer. Jesus has come to tell us who God is and what sort of relationship we can have with God, and there is no other path for us to take. You like to go off by yourself, Pedro, and spend a whole day alone in the hills, admiring nature. And I think that's just fine. That helps you come to an ever better understanding of your task in the world, helps you get into the problem of human reconciliation—Jesus' reason for being. If prayer made you a guru, it wouldn't be Christian prayer.

I've mentioned to you that little book on "spirituality" that our friend had me read. I've told you I don't buy it, and I've told you why. It teaches self-control—how to master your passions, how to overcome all your vices, how to become a perfect, balanced person, safe from all storms from without. This isn't Jesus' ideal. Not that Jesus tells you to give yourself up to all vices, or to be the slave of your passions. But Jesus' special mark is compassion for the world—sorrow that persons failed to love one another, and the desire to give his life so that all may be reconciled to one another. The Christian ideal is certainly not "impassibility"—which means being beyond suffering. On the contrary, it means taking the world drama on oneself.

On the other hand, it is not a desire to suffer for suffering's sake. Just the fact you suffer doesn't make you a Christian. I'd say, instead: if you love, you're a Christian, and because you love, you suffer. Friends of mine have so often criticized me for having refused to get involved with certain Eastern theories and prayer techniques. I'm allergic to all this. You're taught to concentrate on your "self," you're taught prayer as an end in itself. The ideal is to form the "praying human being." No, look in the gospel: the emphasis there is on the formation of the *saving* human being, the altruist—the formation of men and women who take up the great human problem, which is the problem of nonacceptance. This will certainly lead them to suffer and to pray, and to a great deal of joy, because friendship is joy.

Ché Guevara's Bolivian diary is a description of a horrible life, if we take it externally. Living in a forest, surrounded by dangers of every kind, with the threat of death at any moment, without any of the conveniences of modern life—yet there is an optimism there, a spirit, that I'd call Christian in substance. Here are all the vibrations of friendship, hope, and gladness. Life is good for something! All this takes you a long way from the wise indifference of certain Eastern theories for bringing you in out of the rain, out of the storms of life.

Don't let yourself be influenced by those who tell you, Pedro, that prayer isn't worthwhile because we have to change the world in a hurry, because we have to have a revolution. Don't let it bother you when they call you "spiritualistic." Let your prayer feed on a concrete, authentic commitment to building communion, and let prayer light up your desire to build communion and make it ever purer and deeper.

You were curious, Pedro, about what a famous theologian told me one day, one who said he "spoke for the majority." He told me, "You can see by experience that there are far greater differences among persons than merely being rich and being poor. There are sick persons, there are healthy persons, there are beautiful persons, there are ugly persons. This is the will of God! Why all this concern about rich and poor, oppressor and oppressed? This is really only an incidental, unimportant difference!"

Poor us, if those are our theologians! Surely the Reverend Doctor must teach his students that Christ came to take away the sins of the world. Well, how are you going to take away the sins of the world without facing up to the problem of social differences, for which we are responsible? What does sin mean to him if it doesn't mean anticommunion and antilove? Aren't the divisions among us the visible effect of antilove?

We have to be careful not to make prayer a purely intellectual exercise, a kind of playing with words. Prayer is life. Everything that has to do with building a communion of brothers and sisters is prayer. Once I know that the only one who can build communion is God, the logical thing would be for me to meet with and talk it over with God. Once we have conceived a certain mistrust of ourselves, and admit we're capable of betrayal, we have all the more reason for not abandoning prayer. You don't meet with the Lord to unload on him what you should be doing yourself. You meet with him because you're convinced that you too, like thousands, like millions of others, can betray your friends. Pedro, you were with me the other evening in Sanare, out on the street, when a farm worker waved at a gentleman pulling up in a fancy car. No response. And the worker complained: "Remember when he was campaigning for the elections? We thought he was our friend! And now he doesn't even know us!"

You can be convinced you're doing the loving thing, and yet betray someone by what you are doing. Unconsciously you're selfish, domineering, prideful. Unless all women and men discover this basic truth, and become humble in the realization that they can betray their sisters and brothers, and that all the psychiatrists in the world will not save them from their capacity for betrayal—nothing that we do, even if it's good in itself, will have any consequences for liberation. This is all I can tell you about prayer.

The peoples of Latin America are under the yoke of two forces that tend to paralyze their history. One is that of an alienating religion that leads them to a god who has no connection with life. It could be Jupiter, with his terrible thunderbolts, or Mercury the benefactor, who solves our economic problems, or some latter-day wonder-worker who makes up for the shameful paucity of medical services.

The other paralyzing force is the individualistic spiritualism of Latin American intellectuals, with their recipe for peace of soul for those who have no peace. Behind this spiritualism is an astute, intelligent maneuvering to maintain and preserve the opium religion and neutralize the revolutionary, liberating power of the gospel. Not all of those who follow the spiritualistic current have this diabolical intention, I readily admit. The great majority of them are good persons, who find comfort and consolation by having recourse to prayer. They have an abstract political plan that takes no account of the current stage in which Latin America finds itself, and a plan that the masses can't get involved with because they are in no position to understand it. The strategists' language is unintelligible.

We need to discover the force that moves history—discover the secret that gets liberation under way, so that Latin America can then transmit it to the world. *This is the mission of Latin America.* If you see this, and then picture yourself as too small for such an undertaking, and you don't know how to "pull yourself up," then your helplessness becomes an invitation and thrust to prayer. This is where faith is built—in these concrete needs. You, the youth, the younger generation of a Latin America called to renew the Old World and the tired old bourgeois church, are the ones with the mission of finding the way to bring liberation to Latin America and then bring Latin America to the world.

Try calling out to Christ Jesus. Try coming to an understanding with him. I know that it is the Spirit of the Lord, Pedro, more than any words of mine, who will help you not to yield, and will show you the meaning of prayer, without my contaminating you with my intellectualism, which would deprive your relationship with Christ of its authenticity.

11

Being Christian:
A Love Problem

Yo nací en esta ribera
del Arauca vibrador—
soy hermano de la espuma,
de las garzas,
de las rosas, y del sol!

Born was I on this bank
of the trembling Arauca—
brother to the foam,
to the purple herons,
to the roses and the sun!

Sing, Pedro. Never stop singing. After all we've said the moment
has come to shed a little light on a certain magic word you've heard
in our conversations—a word that sounds strange to you, something from another world, something nonhuman: the word "contemplation."

When we've been on walks, and I've seen you looking into the
distance as if enchanted by the panorama you beheld, I've told you
you're a "contemplative." You've told me you'd heard this word
used in a religious sense and your own conclusion was that contemplation must mean looking at God as realistically as you and I were
able to see the landscape that day.

127

Well, yes and no. In religion as we have it, contemplation emerges as a "super-skill," like speaking another language, and a very difficult one, say, Chinese. Not many Westerners learn Chinese. You need a lot of books, an audiovisual cubicle, many hours of study, and then a great deal of liberty to devote yourself to study. Little by little, they become so proficient that they can understand Chinese "on the fly," the way you, Pedro, can understand Venezuelans pursing their lips and nodding one direction or another. According to the situation, that can mean it's going to rain today, or let's go to work up there in the mountains, or I was born over near that ridge. I've had a lot of trouble catching on, and you've gotten a big kick out of my mistakes.

Well, contemplatives are the ones who, after long application and a great deal of effort, have deciphered the difficult language used by human beings in converse with God. And they understand it, Pedro, the way you understand the glossary of Venezuelan nods of the head. This is the concept that has given rise to the communities of contemplatives I've mentioned to you so often. And now there are some modern ones, even in Caracas. They're like judo or karate schools. You're taught how to sit, how to breathe, what to eat, and all the prayer techniques.

This attracts a great many Catholics, even priests, brothers, and sisters, who don't want to be left behind. Look, we say to ourselves, if these schools have so many clients, then why shouldn't we, who've been the prayer experts for centuries now, get modern? And so we too get busy and set up prayer schools.

You have to understand, Pedro, that religious are continually inculcated with the notion that they should be persons of prayer. But they get a rather mistaken idea of prayer. And because they rarely attain the ideal set before them, they carry around within themselves a permanent dissatisfaction, a kind of guilt complex, and they clutch at every opportunity to become "good at" prayer. This explains much of the enthusiasm, especially among nuns, for these new "discoveries" about prayer. And they accept these discoveries without discussion.

If only we would concentrate all the training we do on inculcating a responsibility for evangelizing the world—which means making a murderous world into a communion of sisters and brothers—you'd see how quickly things would change. The main interest would no longer lie in being a "person of prayer," but in being a person who prays, and prays a lot—in being a person of love, a "reconciler."

The "training" type of prayer—prayer by "method"—is obviously for the bourgeois—somebody with the time and money to go to these karate-prayer schools. And even if a man or woman of the people had the time and money, he or she would tell you, "I have something else to do," and this would be a totally serious answer. Given the time and money, the thing to do would be to go and learn judo, to learn to protect yourself! As ever, prayer turns out to be a matter of expertise, and quite a professional one at that, rather than being an encounter with God.

In the gospel, it's clear, very clear, that the guests of honor at the festival of contemplation are the poor. Yes, Doña Juana, Santiago, and little old Eulogio. These are number one. Do you think Eulogio ever turns up at any of these schools? "Prayer-school prayer" is intended for the people, that's true. But it's taught by priests. Priests go to these schools, and the masses get the results secondhand. It's the bourgeois prayer experience—popularized, simplified, made more accessible, but it's still the bourgeois experience. Of course, the Holy Spirit may take this experience in hand and use it to make contemplatives of the people. How do we know that won't happen? Remember, Pedro, the evening I told you we shouldn't laugh at the fat woman who was trying to move her legs and arms in rhythm with that exultant, triumphant song? All human expressions seem to me worthy of respect, and if I look at them with respect, they are most beautiful. The danger is the one we've gone over so many times—attempting to build a communion of brothers and sisters "the easy way." The danger is that of announcing that communion has been built, when it is still to be built.

And indeed the observation made by those who devote themselves to the new prayer style is: Finally we feel good, we feel welcome, we're building communion. Now, I believe that this has to be a very, very important step ahead—to place the accent on a "feeling of well-being in communion," on this burning desire to be sisters and brothers. For human beings to discover that it's good to be together, to discover that encounter is truly happiness, seems to me to be extremely positive. But we Christians must not fall into our habitual idealism—into that silly, phony, uncritical, sterile, antievangelical optimism that says: we're sisters and brothers already! Here is how it would go: " 'See how good it is for brothers and sisters to dwell together in unity'! It's fantastic! And it must be even more beautiful than we think, for so many persons risk their lives, risk torture, persecution, and death in order to build a world of brothers and sisters. So why not bear this evening's joy to all men and women, why not extend it to all the earth?"

But think it over very carefully: this joy cost Jesus the cross, and will always cost the cross. So sing, sing, brothers and sisters! Because you have a long, hard march ahead of you.

God Walking with Us

Well, then, what is contemplation? Contemplation is becoming fully and totally aware that Christ is living in you, Pedro, and that you and he are one. I don't mean one in the somewhat poetic sense in which two friends are "one"—as you heard yesterday that Pedro and Lazaro are "like this," and Luís held up his two fingers together on one hand because Pedro and Lazaro are always together and always talking, talking. Our friendship—friendship between human beings—is most beautiful. But it's limited.

Jesus used examples to express our oneness with him. We read together the one about grafting—the vine and the branches. Saint Paul can't think of how to say it—he talks about one body and one spirit, you're in Jesus and Jesus is in you, as your right and left arms belong to the same body and are alive with the same life, which you might call "Pedro's life." These arms live "on" you and with you, and when you die, they die.

It's a mystery, but not too much of a mystery, because, as I've told you, Pedro, we can actually experience it and feel it. When this aspect of Christian reality is forgotten, our faith dries up. You don't see Christians any more—persons who move, who speak, who love—you see "Christianity." There's hardly any difference between "Aristotelian Christianity" and "Marxist Christianity." Jesus has not left us a legacy of "Christianity," but of Christians, those who live his life.

Renewing Christianity by writing a book about "Christian politics," or renewing prayer, or writing a book on how the religious life ought to be today, means putting new wine in old wineskins, or sewing new material onto an old garment that's ready to be thrown away. We shouldn't be making new theories, we should be making new Christians. These new Christians will find the practical means to build communion.

If we're striking for the root of what it is to be a Christian and we begin to quarrel over theory, we'll be paralyzed. We have to get over defining what it means to be a Christian in terms of doctrine. The Christian is someone grafted onto Jesus and alive with his life. Mistrust of mysticism has removed us from the radical vision of what it is to be a Christian and forced us back on a body of doctrine, so we'll look "up to date" and ready to face the world. I think we ought to be capable today of this naked radicality: the Christian is someone grafted onto Christ. This would make us capable of welcoming projects of renewal, liberation, and communion-building in the world, and yet with an openness that would be free of mistrust, and free of the infatuation that is so typical of Christians. I maintain that it's a much easier and more fertile meeting, a "cleaner" one, when a "mystical Christian"—that is, a real, authentic Christian—meets a Marxist than when an "ideological" Christian does, be the latter ever so modern and open.

Living in Christ, Pedro, living grafted onto Christ, doesn't make you disappear. Your face is still Pedro's, and so is your character. Your friends will always recognize you, in fact they'll see you more and more clearly, because they'll find you more affectionate, more patient, more capable of understanding them, more interested in their problems—they'll recognize you more and more for what you are. If you'd filled your head with doctrine, you'd have become pedantic, boring. That's why I've always dragged my feet when you've asked me to teach you what you should tell your friends. Nothing. You'll know what to say. If you live your life in Christ authentically, others will not say Pedro's a bigot, or a "churchy" kind of guy. You've told me yourself how happy you were to go back to your neighborhood for the weekend, where you were welcomed with affection and true joy. They grilled you, they "stripped" you, as you put it, but they welcomed you as if it were a special holiday. Isn't that so?

To get back to our conversation—the contemplative is someone who becomes aware of this condition of being grafted onto Christ. And you know what I mean by becoming aware. You hear a lot about "conscientization" where you come from. Someone can be poor and oppressed and not know it. That is, someone can not know that this condition is unjust and that it can be transformed. Persons suffer and don't have full awareness of their suffering and don't know how to get out of it. Little by little, as they struggle along the path of liberation, they see that they are oppressed and that they can be liberated. Gradually their minds grow clearer, not by dint of studying, but because they're immersed in life. Contemplatives become conscious of their life in Christ. They are two-in-one. Awareness of it grows clear not in a study hall, but in the midst of life.

The consequences of this awareness are enormous. And it is these consequences that help one see who is a contemplative and who isn't. Using this touchstone, I have often discovered true contemplatives among the poor, in persons who've had no inkling of it. If I told them, "You're a contemplative," they would have looked at me as if I'd told them they were a lawyer or a parachutist. There's no contradiction between what I said before and what I'm saying now, because this intensified consciousness doesn't bear on whether or not you're a contemplative, it bears on having God with you.

One day, in a Latin American country—I'll tell you the truth, she didn't have so much as an old blanket to wrap him in—a poor woman asked me to baptize her baby. I asked her what baptism meant to her. Her answer: *God walks with us.* This is what I mean by an awareness of our grafting into Christ Jesus—which is different from the reflexive consciousness of being a contemplative.

If I had to sum up all these consequences—which we can call "signs"—in one concept, they mean: resembling Christ. Your mother, Pedro, looks like your grandpa, and you look like your mother, so much so that when you went back to your neighborhood many persons recognized you at first glance.

There are two characteristics Jesus has that one recognizes right away: passion for his Father and passion for human beings. After all, he is the son of his Father and the brother of all men and women. For a contemplative, this passion for the Father translates into a clear awareness of being loved with a love that can never be plumbed to its depths. And Jesus' love for his brothers and sisters is not a "generic" love. It's a specific type. It's the kind that drives him to "take the form of a slave." Noncontemplatives—those not possessed of the Spirit—discuss, "from the outside," how Jesus lived, if he was middle class or lower class, if he lived on roots or ate platefuls of meat, if he'd drive a Rolls or an old Volkswagen today or maybe just hoof it. Those who have the Spirit of the Lord have no need of discussion, because they are completely caught up in a desire to take the *form of a slave.*

As in Jesus' time, humanity today is divided into oppressed and oppressors, slaves and free. Jesus came to the oppressed, to slaves. This may seem too simple, but it's a fact. It could even be called a "scientific" way of looking at reality. Tuberculosis existed in Roman times; but they called the disease "chest weakness," and didn't well understand what it was. Today we know it and define it. So it is with the "oppressed."

Signs of the Contemplative

The sign of the contemplative, Pedro, will always be poverty. No, excuse me—how many times have I told you that poverty should not be spoken of, that it doesn't exist! The sign of the contemplative is this, and it's unmistakable: you'll always find the contemplative mingling with the oppressed, with slaves.

From within the condition of slavery and oppression, Jesus sought to rebuild the two elements of dignity that human beings had culpably lost: freedom and communion. Men and women have made themselves slaves, and therefore they are no longer brothers and sisters. This is something the best of human beings have always agreed on. (Well, they may tell you they don't agree about the "culpably lost" part. But they will tell you: right, the two elements to go looking for are freedom and communion.)

You'll always find the ones with the Spirit of the Lord on the side of the victims, Pedro. And don't be swayed by all the beautiful speeches. We religious, especially, are incredibly good at giving beautiful defensive speeches. We avoid certain inconvenient simplifications, and, on the pretext of clarity and precision, fish in murky waters.

The mighty, too, are servants. The heads of political parties, presidents of republics—aren't they servants of the people? And the wives of affluent capitalists, bound to their awful social obligations—are they not slaves?

It's clear that the "slavery of Jesus" has not been adopted, because all decisions are taken in favor of oppressors—the mighty, not the lowly. They'll try to mix you up by telling you, "Not everyone can live in a pasteboard shack. If they did, we'd still be back in the stone age."

Never lose the sensitivity of the people's way of reasoning. With it you're able to suddenly detect, in someone's speech or way of acting, "This person isn't one of us." This person hasn't embraced the cause of the oppressed, the poor. These are the ones who toil and live to maintain oppression, not to demolish it and transform it into communion.

Christ did not come to proclaim himself the universal brother, as certain persons do who hold meetings and, sickened by the phenomenon of racial discrimination, declare themselves universal brothers and sisters, citizens of the world. They deny the existence of black and white. Christ came to create a communion of sisters and brothers, not to proclaim it. If you proclaim it, you can even dress in sackcloth and let yourself be infested with fleas, you won't "bother" anyone. In fact, the poorer you are, and the more spectacular your poverty, the more you'll be pitied, especially by the bourgeois. But if you set out to build communion, to join the oppressed and point your finger at oppressors, one way or another you'll finish on a cross.

The contemplative is someone who has drunk the cup of joy and sorrow to the dregs. If we saw reality without its cloak of appearances (as we shall never be able to see it), no one would be able to say to a contemplative: "I've had more enjoyment than you have," or "I've suffered more than you have." You see, contemplatives have discovered the tenderness of the Father, and they see it in all its particulars, from things inside their own lives to external things, like stars, flowers, water, or the sun. Artists give us a very pale, imperfect image of what a person can discover and enjoy in the contemplation of nature. Between Saint Francis and Rembrandt or Picasso there is a great gulf.

But remember, Pedro, contemplation increases the pain of communion unattained, the pain of the injustice inflicted on the poor and the oppressed. It will increase your interior suffering, Pedro, if you become a contemplative. You will be more persecuted and misunderstood. Your struggles will multiply. I'm reminded of the mother of the two apostles, James and John. She wanted her sons to be happy and at peace (one was a bit on the wild side, and she hoped he'd settle down), so she asked Jesus to keep them close always, close to himself, one on his right and the other on his left. But Jesus told her that this would not be a guarantee of comfort. They were going to have to drink the cup that he was going to drink.

The contemplative is someone in whom Jesus relives all his tender, dramatic love, a love that enjoys the beauty of a field of flowers and then lets itself be captured and abused by Pilate's henchmen and raised up on the cross. Suppose your neighborhood friends, your mother, and your sisters and brothers, were to say: "Pedro's crazy. He could have been better off, and he lives the life of the poor. He had a light, easy job and now he works like a dog. He was looking for a nice life and see what he got!" That would be a good sign. But if they had to say: "Pedro's a sly one! He's gone off and has the easy life. He has a beautiful house, with every convenience. He has cronies to take care of all his affairs; he doesn't have to worry about a thing." That, Pedro, would mean the Lord Jesus is gone. He stopped, he knocked, but then he went on.

I'd like to talk to you, Pedro, about another aspect of contemplation. You know, something has occurred to me as I consider your youthfulness. Arturo, I say to myself, sooner than you think, you'll be old and useless. Time is putting you on the shelf. You'll be "contemporary" no longer. You'll be speaking of the past as if it were the present. Your watch will stop like the old doctor's watch in *Wild Strawberries*, and you'll say, "It's nine o'clock," and it'll be nine o'clock, all right, but nine o'clock, June 16, 1986, not nine o'clock, June 16, 1940, and everything you say will be out of place and out of synch. And I thought of all the invalids, all the peasant women who spend their whole lives at home having children and raising them and seeing them leave—all those who can't build communion by political means. I thought of little Juan, perfectly sane at first but in a mental hospital now, in the tragic awareness of being of no use to anyone on the face of the earth. Has Jesus abandoned this mass of humanity—Jesus who is so attached to everyone and loves each of us personally? Would he who came to destroy marginalization marginalize whole groups of men and women?

I thought and I thought, and I rediscovered a dimension of my faith that I have to confess, Pedro, was all but covered with dust. These persons may not represent political forces—but they are historical forces, in the sense that, mysteriously, they move history toward a communion of sisters and brothers. Words and political commitment aren't the only things that help communion. There's the cross and martyrdom of Christ, too, fecundating all human suffering. It's hard—maybe impossible—for us to see "how" and "why." Everyone, even an atheist, will acknowledge that it's not useless to spend twenty years in prison for the cause of liberation. It's not useless to die by firing squad or be tortured to death for freedom and communion.

For an atheist, such sufferings may be forces in history in the sense that they serve as a call and challenge. All, regardless of the ideology that they embrace, think that such persons, rendered useless politically, influence history in a very important way. And they immortalize them in monuments, to make them speak, make them "get through to" others, summoning them to join the struggle for the triumph of truth. But atheists deny that these persons have any influence beyond the power of example. And when a "useless suffering" comes home to roost, they're dumbfounded, they give up hope.

We Christians, without having a great deal more lucidity, believe in a further, more direct effectiveness. The powerful force thrusting history forward, without respite, toward freedom and communion, this mysterious force that, despite failures and seeming uselessness, sustains the person who has hope, comes from the cross of Christ, Christ alive again today in a thousand ways, in us, in our suffering. You don't have all that much choice. Your option for Christ impels you to concrete choices in life. If you know that your own manner of building community is political, you can't choose the path your mother trod—she who had to accept the life she was given, in lowly, silent sacrfice.

It may be that to her silence and patient acceptance you owe your awakening—your feeling that your life should serve for some useful purpose, that it should weigh on the plus side of the scales of history. Obviously there is a mystery in history, an "imponderable," hidden force.

We have not yet found all the answers. It may be that by discovering the concurrence of all forces and all laws that give rise to life, one day we shall be able to reproduce life, as certain sporadic experiments suggest. We cannot set advance limits to human inventiveness and creativity. Experience has given the lie to any number of "impossibilities."

But I think we shall never be able to answer the question, "What is life?" in an exhaustive manner. After all, whatever men and women do, think, and create, is the exercise of their existence. It begins with their existing. They can turn around and imagine the "nothing" that precedes them, this empty space, as it were, preceding their existence—but they discover that this "nothing" is "nothing" for someone who can think of a nothing, and hence for a person who exists, who has life, who can think of life.

But this is philosophy. Sorry, Pedro, I slipped. But don't you complicate your life. Only, as a Christian, think no one useless, and remember that no one can say with certitude who most moves history, and thus is really more important—the secretary general of the United Nations, or Agustín who knows only his work in the fields, his Sunday *palito* ("shot glass"), and that simple gladness he shares with us when he comes to visit. If we wanted to do a little reasoning and enter into the mystery, we would come to see that these persons are historical forces, because they generate the vital energy called love.

Evangelizing by Loving

All our conversations, which to the reader will seem to be between two persons, actually are more like choral pieces. And they have brought us to this conclusion: that being a Christian is not a problem of the will, or of instruction, but of love. Christians are persons who discover that they are loved, and find that the best response they can give, the only way to say "thanks" for the love they receive, is the response of loving. The very need to love leads them not to refuse any proposal, any path that seems to them to be a good one for building communion. At the same time, the very need to love prevents you from shutting yourself up in an ideology, regardless of whether the ideology might happen to be Christian. If you really love, if you've been captured by the love of Christ, you throw yourself into the battle for communion, but you're on the lookout not to lose the essential thing: love for human beings. The problem is difficult, and we can't escape it.

Today the paper from Caracas, *El Nacional*, reports some statements by the Soviet premier. Here's someone who's not religious, or at least claims to be an atheist. And he proposes that all the powers sign an agreement outlawing "new types of weapons of mass destruction." Without saying that the arms in question already exist, he is stating that modern technology has progressed to the point where there seems to be the grave danger that weapons could be produced that are even more terrible than the nuclear ones we have already. The newspaper account concludes with an observation by some Western diplomats that the Soviet statement was directed especially at the United States, which has always led the Soviet Union in the arms race.

This Soviet proposal, though it makes sense, is very naive. It's naive in the same way so many sermons on peace are naive. Even supposing that it's sincere, if we go to the root of the thinking behind it, this is what we find: "Human beings, why don't you like one another? Instead of butchering one another, why don't you try being friends? How fine a place the world would be if we exchanged Swiss chocolate instead of nuclear weapons!"

One would think that everything could be straightened out if only everyone wished it so. We can all see the monstrous consequences when someone is not actually free to love and yet is called on to act as if he or she were free. Human beings are unable to love, and the result of an inability to love neighbors, spouses, and friends is that we end up with nuclear and postnuclear weaponry. And the destruction of humanity seems right around the corner.

Put yourself in the Soviet premier's shoes. What more could he say? Disarm! The answer will of course be yes, and of course that will mean no, and the arms race will continue unabated. Is there any remedy in sight? Are we headed for destruction? I don't believe we are.

Will men and women open their eyes and see that they are loved? The Franciscan movement was possible because the population of Europe was much lower then and the wars between cities were not very destructive. I can see this evangelization of love moving a *little* European world. Could the miracle be repeated today? I don't know, Pedro. I'm not a prophet.

One thing is sure: in order to be believed, today's preachers of the gospel will have to offer concrete proof that their love for men and women is not abstract, is not made of words divorced from ongoing history.

For women and men of past generations, freedom was a privilege, a right that had to be won—the right to vote, the right to profess one's own religion, the right to property, and so on. For them freedom was the acknowledgment of these rights. And for such acknowledgments men and women struggled and died.

Today freedom seems to me more like a force and quality within a human being. The "unfree" human being is the one who, for various reasons, is unable to love—that is, is unable to live in a peaceful relationship with others and with things; the aggressive, violent, destructive, cynical, inhibited type. I could draw various sketches but all of them would come down to this: the person unable to love is the person who is not free, and who therefore projects signs of unfreedom into all his or her decisions. The Soviet premier's proposal is valid as addressed to free men and women. But as addressed to unfree men and women it is not valid. It's like inviting persons restricted to wheelchairs, "Let's go out for a walk."

It will take a mighty burst of the energy of love to liberate human beings in time to get them to stop concentrating on weapons to destroy their sisters and brothers and concentrate instead on the ideal of peaceful coexistence. We Christians believe that only Christ can give human beings this kind of freedom, the kind that goes to the root, that is unseen, but is the foundation of all other freedoms and all decisions for coexistence. This is why Jesus talked about salt, leaven, light. It's a freedom "on the inside," and it's the prime freedom, coming before all the others. Involvement in political and economic liberation is an exercise of this personal freedom, the ability to love that only Jesus can give us. Once you have this freedom, you use ideology as a tool—but you don't let yourself be used, because you feel, deep inside, that the only absolute is love for human beings.

I'll try to explain what I mean in an understandable way, Pedro. To actualize communion in Bojó, we'd have to get rid of the distinction between landholders and day laborers, those who own the land and those who work it. All would have to be in the same condition. Not all would have the same amount of money—it's not a matter of total equality—but there shouldn't be exploiters and exploited.

To reach this point, men and women find theories that "rationalize"—make logical—this right, and they try to turn their theories into practice and reality in life. These theories are called the "ideology" needed to actualize communion. The combat is not waged with sticks and guns alone. It's waged principally with ideas. And even the battles of sticks and guns are set up by ideas. And God grant that there be no more talk of sticks and guns—that ideas alone remain!

But at a certain point, ideology can interest me so much and absorb me so much that human beings interest me no longer. Now it's the ideology that interests me, like a great game, chess, for example, which I've become terrifically good at.

Here's the main difference between the bourgeois and the poor. The bourgeois are able to appreciate only ideology. They're so far removed from persons that for them ideology becomes all. The poor turn to those who have well contrived plans. This is where they are vulnerable. This is where they can be, and are, betrayed. But what else can they do? And so, from one oppression, they fall under another. One way or another, they think, it's worth it, because it's a gain, it's a step ahead.

Those who work out plans generally don't love. They look more to the verification of their ideas, they seek the triumph of these plans, this ideology, rather than true liberation. And, alas, all liberations leave behind a residue of evil, unlove, uncommunion, and delusion, and seem to make human aggressiveness ever more threatening. A communion of brothers and sisters is not proliferating in the world.

This happens in politics, art, religion—wherever and whenever we lose sight of our neighbors, our peers, to fall in love with ideas. The poor don't succumb to this. It is possible only with the bourgeois. The poor can fall victim to the cunning of the ideologues. They can be victimized by it. The ideologues can oppress them with it. But if you stay on the side of the people and let yourself be governed and guided by the community, if your love for persons is authentic, if you experience liberation, you can be sure you haven't fallen into ideology and aren't betraying your sisters and brothers. Jesus is forever denouncing two types of persons, who seem very similar to one another: the rich and the Pharisees, those who do not know how to love.

The Pharisees are the ideologues—those who have turned religion into a system of obedience to ever more complex cultural traditions, instead of an encounter with God. The rich are the practical ideologues—those who place their trust in money, in the *symbol* of exchange and communication, rather than in actual communication. The Pharisee is the theoretical ideologue, who trusts in ideas, plans, and projects instead of persons. Pharisees think that rules produce life. They don't realize that rules are born of life and the threat of death. There is a perpetual antagonism between rule, law, and life.

I wonder, Pedro, when I read my notes from my dialogue with you and others, why I'll be publishing this dialogue instead of burning my notebook. But my notebook has grown dear to me. It reflects a life lived in community—not ideas as such, but a life in common. You, Pedro, are a nearby reality, and a symbol. You are the symbol of a category of youth who'd like to know how to speak, and how to figure out my life. They're young persons like you, of the people, of the ghetto, who have not suffered the harm of an ideological training. They've suffered other damage, of course, and we've had something of a look at this. There's no such thing as an undamaged person. Everyone we meet is a damaged person, someone in urgent and absolute need of freedom.

Ideologues are tempted to take damaged persons out of circulation and keep them in a museum, like paintings too long exposed to dust, humidity, and changes in the weather. In the museum, it often happens that a restorer will see a painting shining like new again and say, "Why send it back out to suffer the pains of the past?" And so they keep it in the museum workshop and feed it vitamins. This also happens in the Christian world. When they see you've been harmed, too much harmed, they fix you up, then they put you out of circulation and make you a "museum piece."

I've been afraid this might happen to you, Pedro. So I'm content to suffer the sorrow of seeing you leave. We'll be separated, after a prolonged joint life of "tasty" (to use your word) encounters and collisions. And you've been the one to tell me, your teacher in the faith, that separation will be no obstacle to either friendship or communion. On the contrary, with distance, the dross of paternalism, aggressiveness, and the unconscious quest of affective satisfaction is removed. I'm summarizing your long, touching discourse of the eve of your departure, and of course my words are not yours. But I believe I've been faithful to your meaning.

12

The Church, an "Expert on the Human Being"?

Here I am, alone with my manuscript, confronted with the task of typing it up (and I'm not much of a typist). And I wonder if I ought to do it. Saint Francis and the first Franciscans certainly didn't spring forth from the reading of a book. A book can inspire decisions, provided it doesn't attempt to furnish a precise model or recipe. At best it can supply a kind of minimal check: that what one is thinking is not pure foolishness.

How many persons I've met who have told me, "When I read that book of yours, I thought I must not be crazy after all or at least not the only crazy one." This isn't what's so much on my mind, actually—there are stronger stimulants and more up-to-date ones—I'm thinking rather of the responsibility one has to one's readers: that of communicating the alternation of discoveries and corrections.

I'm making a discovery, perhaps a little late, of the absolute importance of praxis, and of the absolute urgency of changing our methods—demolishing our old methods. The gospel *needs a long season of freedom* to manifest itself and once more become a force in history. The church has called itself an "expert on the human being." This is perhaps the most dangerous phrase to have emerged from Vatican II. If it had expressed a humble desire, it would have been beautiful. Basically this is Christianity's real nostalgia, the point toward which the Christian task has always been directed: to become an expert on the human being. But I'm afraid it may have been pure declamation, and that would be dangerous. Actually the church is not an expert on the human being. It's an expert in a certain anthropology. It's an expert on the human being stuck on a pin like a butterfly.

The "experience" of the human being through an analysis of the "person" and personal relationships, an analysis of what the person should be, swaddled in Scholastic terminology, has come down to us carried along by an ever skimpier trickle of thought, an ever diminishing current. This experience of the human being has not improved a great deal at the hands of Freudian or Marxist contributions, filtered as these have been through our "essentialistic" training, which is incapable of grasping the creativity of the negative, the contradictory, the hypothetical. We like things clear. We like to have our feet on the ground. We like risk-free investments. We like life in its epilogue, not life in the act of its own birth.

The church has always had the tendency to welcome "converts" and put them to work, as it has welcomed (and this is its better side, covering the other) the deaf, the dumb, the blind, the lame, the leprous. But conversions are often an attempt to reject history. They are sincere when this rejection is the rejection of a pernicious element in history, the element of anticommunion. Then it's not so much a rejection as it is an option for something seen as more essential. Even when it's absolutely and totally negative, and simply springs from delusion, it may still constitute a negation of a pernicious element in history, and then conversion is fertile, and therefore fecundating.

To return to what I was telling Pedro, these persons may not have a political role, but they have a historical role. Charles de Foucauld comes to mind. He inspires choices that he might not have made himself, but they are certainly inspired by his courageous withdrawal to the Sahara. We cannot be certain that there was no fear in his movement of flight and withdrawal, fear of failing to move about in a "new" world with the skill of an expert. Evangelical life was more complex and difficult than the life he had earlier followed in lawless simplicity. Nor may we say that his flight contained no element of perfectionism. But the important thing is that he discovered the importance of fellowship with the Muslim Tuaregs on *their* terms, and he opened up an enormous territory to be traversed by those who choose to follow the trail he blazed.

"Converts" are not sincere when they ask of the church a role that seems to be the same they had before, perhaps even more important, but protected from the vicissitudes of history. They are not willing to dismount, even if the "new steed" is a wooden horse.

If the church wants to be an expert on the human being, it will have to be an expert on history, because the human being is history and history is made by the human being. Vatican II opened up horizons of hope, erected important signposts, brought to the surface nostalgia and pain that had been afflicting the church for centuries. Now we saw the church of the poor, its nonpresence in the working world, the cry for freedom, acceptance of all that human beings create, believe, and seek, however wrapped in ambiguity. Its journey is more like a groping forward on a moonless night than Saint John's walking in the light. It is an open dialogue with all men and women, without discrimination against any religion. It is friendship as a climate of relationships. It is the people of God now "sacralized" in its capacity as a people and therefore desacralized. It is the religious life as the prophetic life, and hence a life capable of challenging what the institution has crystallized and elevated to the rank of "absolute"—hence also ready for persecution, incomprehension, and stoning, the price of propheticism.

Vatican II does not not transmit to "religious life" the challenge to dig a $20,000 swimming pool, but to be prophetic, which is a little different. And the church's journey is other things besides, bearing the dreams of our youth ever higher, ever beyond the "now." Since the council there has been only one "right attitude"— that of silence and waiting. The best service we the clergy can render is that of keeping silent and waiting.

Pedro is gone. I'm alone with my notebook. And I want to justify myself. This justification will be an attempt to explain why I'm publishing these notes. The council proposes to the world that it observe the church and judge it. This is the end of a long story of two groups that have lived in mutual isolation: one lives on a beautiful country estate, but totally out of touch with the times, wastefully enjoying long periods of sloth. The other group lives in a less poetic apartment in town, a residence less burdened with the past and more functional, more adapted to working persons who seek to have as short as possible a distance to commute. The two groups decide to live together. The thing to be sacrificed is the country estate. At first the country group seems relieved to leave the house of memories with the prospect of being together with others, and at last being useful persons. They're leaving the estate with some sorrow, but also with hope and optimism. They're not headed for retirement, uselessness, and senility; they're headed for life. And life will be hard and implacable, but it will be life. The decision to join the two groups together was accepted unanimously, and it was decisive. The long history of their separation was coming to a close. Initiative—not government by fiat—would be in the hands of the "town group." But to reach this point, the "country group," the church, which was receiving a message from the Holy Spirit, had to be a converted church. The hierarchy receiving the message had to be capable of conversion, which would appear to all in the form of trust, hope, and patience.

Forgiveness Is Easy: It's Understanding That's Hard

The father who, in Saint Luke's unforgettable mural, rushes out to greet his profligate son, could have awaited him without a converted heart. He could have awaited him as a needed farm hand, or in the pride of having the neighbors see that his children needed him, or in order to vent his rage and dramatically show that it was he who had been right once again.

We've always focused on the son's conversion, because we've read the parable with an impassible, immobile, unconvertible Aristotelian God in mind. All the movement has been in the son. If instead we had had a mind-set governed by the incarnation—by a God who comes to take on all the affective, emotional richness, the full measure of humanness, which basically is of God, is "truly God's"—we would have grasped the whole meaning of the parable.

The father gives the son his forgiveness, but the son gives the father a new relationship. Parenthood is a relationship, and a relationship is never determined by just one of its terms. This I should like to preach on my knees to all the hierarchs of the church who have had such an astonishing capacity for monologue.

When we come to realize, perhaps in the next life, that the human being is not a secondary appendage of creation, we shall understand how much time we have lost in discussing whether human beings could have been or not been, whether the presence of the human being altered the eternal, absolute, and immutable felicity of God—whether God would have been the same without humankind. When we see that the human being is not a distraction to God, an unnecessary afterthought—as a certain school of speculation, derived from Aristotle, would like to demonstrate to us—then at last the gospel will be vindicated. It will come to light that the deepest, tenderest, most painfully wounded parenthood on earth is but the palest reflection of the resolute and zealous parenthood of God. The father in Saint Luke's drama goes out to meet his son with a heart free of desire for revenge or spirit of proprietorship. "What's mine is yours," he says to the elder son. With him returned, things are different now: parent and child are two friends, ready to walk the same path and share the same goods.

The direction taken by Vatican II presupposes a different "existential" situation. The council has not given us only ideas. First and foremost it has mapped out a change in the church-world relationship. The relationship between hierarchy and people of God, between salvation and history, is different now. The center of this relationship is the heart of the human being. It would be naive to think that, just because there has been a council, the heart of the human being would cease its old habit of damming up the power of God. The problem of our misuse of freedom could not be canceled by the council. And so the church has continued to read, and will continue to read, the message of the council with a preconciliar heart, at least in the generalities of its message. And this causes deep dissonances, dramatic crises, and confusion of language. At times the overtones are comical. The changes of relationship are heard in an ideological key. Practical decisions are remolded into theories—crystal-clear theories, to be sure, but still theories.

I might put it in a nutshell by turning Marx's celebrated maxim inside out: the philosophers have told us how to understand the world, now we must change it, said Marx. Well, the Holy Spirit has sought to change the world, the church, the church-world relationship; now we must discover the theory of this change. The father of the prodigal son, instead of receiving him, calls a solemn meeting of all of the fathers of the region to discuss how to deal with their prodigal children. But there are different opinions. So they decide to meet again. They set up subcommittees for study. One committee will meet periodically, draw up minutes, study them, and propose new projects. The dossier grows heftier and more complete: "How to Receive Prodigals." No one stops to think that it will be the *prodigal* who will have to solve the problem, and that the simplest thing would have been to take the prodigal by the arm and say, "Come on, young man, let's go, don't hurt your father any more, maybe he needs you more than you need him. You can change him, convert him from his severity, his greed, his smugness, his self-assurance. Everything will vanish in an embrace, and you'll be friends again."

What a joke, to think that four hundred years of division—to speak only of the last quarrel, the last "running away from home"—might conclude like a sentimental novel, with the mending of a relationship considered to have been broken by a conscious declaration of unfriendship. Poppycock! These four centuries have not been filled with wailing, and the desire to embrace again. They have been filled with ideology invoked to bolster parental rights, with juridical consultations calculated to augment the distance, with arguments of reason.

The drama of the church is the drama of its radical inability to read history apart from eternal, absolute categories, many removed from time and life. And this translates in practice as a radical mistrust of the human being, of human initiative, and of the human quest—however it may be expressed in the language precisely of trust in human being.

It's easy to forgive. Forgiveness enhances authority, renders the parental role visible, strong, and important. To understand is terribly hard. To understand, you have to share the responsibility, share the blame. The parent-child relationship is created by nature, fed by pride, and given its basis and root by the instinct of ownership. It is given shape by the instincts that maintain us in slavery— the instincts to prevail, to have, to be mighty. Friendship is a sign of freedom, and it is possible only among persons en route to their liberation. The same relationships of parent and child, man and woman, ruler and ruled, church and world, can be lived in a servile parent/child duality or in a parent/child duality become friendship. The message of the "Jerusalem on high"—as Saint Paul would say—which is basically the message of the council, has come to a church in slavery.

The church "pricked up its ears," but now it has translated into ideological terms a message whose main call was for a change in relationships. That's the nub of the problem. Jesus' encounter with the world of the Pharisees comes down to this: ideologically, he and they agree. Jesus has not come to change a single jot or title. Jesus is a free person talking to a group of slaves who have found their comfort and peace in slavery. They are on different frequencies: they say the same things, but they will never agree with one other. The prostitutes and publicans can come to hate their slavery, because it's dirty, it's obscene, it's uncomfortable, it's humiliating. And right in their repudiation of slavery is a spark of freedom. This puts the message of Christ on the airwaves. The Pharisees cannot come to hate their slavery. It's psychologically impossible. They'd have to renounce their existence as Pharisees, and Jesus tells Nicodemus so.

Where the Council Was Heading

We might ask ourselves: If this conversion, this miracle, happened—if the Pharisaical heart were to die out—what would remain of the church? Why, it would become the group of seventy-two disciples sent as lambs into the midst of wolves, with neither purse nor sandals, without diplomacy. "Greet no one on the way!" This is certainly the opposite of the diplomatic protocol that says greet everyone, grin at those who should make us want to throw up! It can't be done. An immense multitude cling to this security for their very lives, cling to a "clear interpretation"—clear in ideas, at any rate. And we have to ask ourselves if this multitude, this crowd, does not include those whom Jesus has forbidden us to scandalize in the figure of the bruised reed and smoking flax. I really don't know. These are questions that continually come to my mind. You can't live in the church without being assailed by questions of this kind.

One thing is certain for me: what the Holy Spirit has asked of the church will be done by the little groups that will always suffice to guarantee the vitality of the church. And this is the way it will be to the end of the world. I thought that the approach of old age might make me pessimistic and bitter. Instead, I peacefully notice that I'm turning into a realist, and a serene one. No longer do I beat my head against the wall. The wall will never crumble. I try to trust in the little group gathered on the bank of the Jordan—not to oppose the kingdom but to give it a new start. John the Baptist teaches today's Christian many things, especially about the coming of spring, the reopening of an old road.

I hear the great choice proposed once more, in polemical, exclusive terms: either to be "normal" persons, who accept history with its ambiguities and try to push it further ahead, keeping account of reality, resigned in advance to the fact that they will never arrive at an omega point, perfection—or to retreat among the lions, beating their breast with a stone and living on water and wild herbs.

Perhaps we expected too much from the council. The council could offer no more than a sketch of what the church ought to be, a kind of blueprint of the kingdom. Some will read this blueprint ideologically, others will read it like babies (the church is full of babies going on seventy), others will read it as adults. These concepts are in Saint Paul, who speaks of children, carnal adults, and spiritual adults. The confusion arises from the fact that "carnal" has come to mean lustful or gluttonous—bodily satisfaction without thought for anything beyond—whereas for Saint Paul an ideology can be carnal, fleshly. Bossuet's lapidary maxim comes to mind: "I made you spiritual in the flesh, and you have become carnal in the spirit."

John's austere withdrawal to the banks of the Jordan is neither flight, nor ideological refuge, nor some form of mystical delirium. His is total dissent, radical, implacable refusal—but deeply loving and rooted in a consecration to the kingdom. Our whole ideological training is anything but training for dissent. It is training for an obedience that knows only one name for all forms of critical reaction: disobedience. It is training for an obedience that is simply a disguise for passivity and indifference. The bishops gathered in Medellín had a moment of courage, and acknowledged this. But they were unable to carry their discourse to its ultimate conclusions. If they had, they'd have seen swarms of bees abandoning their cells to wreak cruel vengeance on the disturbers of their work of relishing the blossoms and making honey!

Disobedience makes noise, and gleams like a lamp, but ends in the desperate acceptance of what looks historical because it's in time; but it isn't historical, because it's cut off from becoming.

Disobedience fails to bear the signs of a creative, human presence. To "be like everyone else," to refuse to be an "exception," and to "follow the rule"—the monotonous formula of run-of-the-mill priests and nuns—can be a sign of modesty, of psychic healthiness, and of acceptance of the position assigned in history to each man and woman. And obviously when one moves out of one's assigned position, one becomes dangerous in any society. Our ideological training permits us no escape from this dilemma: obedience or disobedience. But between the two—one as an intermediate, conciliatory position, but as a position of another kind—stands prophecy.

Vatican II has transmitted this intuition to us too. But prophecy is a risky undertaking. It will not be bridled by ideology or mortified by obedience. The council confirms the notion that the schools of the church aren't schools of prophecy, but of law and legalism, of a speculative theology that I might call "positivist." They aren't schools of courage, but of acquiescence.

A loving dissent is difficult. It is possible only on two conditions: poverty and a profound "interestedness" that merits the name of love. The Baptist's outstanding traits are precisely poverty and tenderness. He quivers with indignation. He throbs with friendship. He brandishes the ax to prune the tree, but he is sure that the vitality of the tree will make it bud anew. His eyes shine with tender, smiling love when a friend appears amid the crowd of penitents. Then these same eyes fix with their steel gaze on the walls of Jerusalem, enclosing a brood of vipers, men of hard, insensitive hearts. Poverty and friendship are the two dialectical terms that join as one in prophecy.

Once in a meeting with religious priests and brothers I sought in vain to show them the relationship between poverty and friendship. They didn't understand me. It was as if I'd said that for good indigestion you have to be in a room painted green. But how can you have the freedom to make disinterested choices without poverty? Choice and exclusion are falsified unless they're guided by a deep affectivity, by an ability to open one's heart of flesh to the depths.

You must choose between things and persons as your masters. If it's to be things, then you put all ideas, schemata, reified immaterialities, even friendship, in their respective pigeonholes, like music put into cassettes. Prophecy takes up its stand outside the walls of the cold, discriminating ideology that gains its clarity by separating itself from ongoing history. Prophecy will not appear in an anonymous, depersonalized "charity" that views women and men like peas in a pod, fails to see them in the interplay of conditions, and at bottom serves to maintain itself in an air-conditioned room, immune to seasonal changes.

Prophecy is a love that separates, that pits three against two, parent against child, and family member against family member. It lights a fire in the cold, and works with a scraper where a lack of novelty has encrusted everything with ice.

Woe to those who vaunt their ideology as "prophecy"! Christ acknowledges that prophecy grows in the Pharisees' garden (John 11:51). But it is quickly transplanted to Gethsemane, to the Jordan, to Calvary. We have all fallen into the fallacy of reading prophecy through ideological lenses. This explains the crises, the discouragements, and so many babyish hopes, hopes not articulated in the hope of "faith, hope, and love." And so we have cried out, time and time again: "Christ has come!"—instead of "Christ is coming!"

All of this had to happen. Prophecy had to find its true throne, which is not in the houses of "kings." After a sojourn in the "Olympus of Michelangelo," prophecy had to don its simple tunic again and return to the banks of the Jordan. The function of prophecy is to proclaim things yet to come, not to enjoy the spoils of victory.

The council went against itself. It had to reinvest the prophetical capital that the Holy Spirit had accumulated within it, but which had come to be entrusted to guardians mostly preoccupied with defensive formulas. The council had to invest this prophetical capital, and the conciliar fathers failed to grasp that what transpired through them did not belong to them but to others. They were unprepared to be a "voice crying in the wilderness."

In the gospel I find an attention to others that is Pharisaical, and hence murderous, and an attention to others that is liberating. Jesus' loving attention to the Canaanite woman, the poor, and the lowly, to whom the Father reveals the secrets of the kingdom, his attention to the prostitute who welcomed him in the house of Simon the Pharisee, was of the liberative type. Jesus has taught us a kind of marveling at others that is a sign that we're healed of envy, of self-sufficiency, of all the ills of a distorted ego. This poor ego of ours exalts itself, deflates itself, flits about, despairs, loses heart, rises again, plays every role on the *dramatis personae*—and never manages to liberate itself in discovery of and admiration for others.

This is the basic affliction targeted by Jesus in two forms of pathological smugness: that of the Pharisees and that of the rich. The Pharisees have no need of others, no need of corroboration. The rich have no need of others, no need of collaboration. At bottom, both forms of self-sufficiency are negations of friendship. It is so obvious that these two are the same side of the coin of the same illness! Here are those who are all closed up in themselves and hence incapable of "catching others on the fly" as they whisk by and offer an opportunity for admiration, as well as an opportunity for collaboration, co-creation. The Pharisee is incapable of admiration, of genuine trust in others. The rich are radically incapable of co-creation, joint management.

Once we have rescued the gospel from its cultural wrappings, we realize that it is a harsh polemic against self-sufficiency, antifriendship. The gospel, however you look at it, is a message of friendship. This is the real cause of crises in religious communities. They have not been able to nurture true friendship. Why? Because they have been infested with the disease of the two self-sufficiencies: phariseeism and creature comfort. They can escape via either route: admiration or co-creation.

Jesus gazes out on the world of the poor, the marginalized. He gazes on that world of manual workers, the world of bootblacks, factotums, and street-sweepers. But he doesn't go there for their services. He goes there to find the place of the revelation of the secrets of the Father. It is there that he finds his collaborators. They know everything about him, including his weaknesses, which scandalize those who hold to an idealistic, unrealistic notion of the human being. If a bigger and bigger part of the church comes to understand this, we're saved.

Admiration and Co-creation

Viewed as a unit, humanity will be neither saved nor lost. Society will always be composed of Pharisees and prophets, those who kill and those who die. My hair has turned white in my quest to resign myself to this philosophy. At times I suspected myself of brushing with conformism—that malady of old age that reaches the brain and the heart. But I think the church is neither dying nor rising. God has accepted the church and history as they are.

Saint Augustine sometimes expressed himself in a somewhat simplistic, Manichean way. Having once been a Manichean himself, its influence hounded him. The wicked exist to make the good good. Were it not for the wicked, how could the good recognize one another? But if we attempt to put more depth and scientific consistency in our examination of this church, in which Pharisees and prophets always run along the same track, in a combat in which there are no victories, if we look at this world in its state of accelerated change and irritating torpor, we shall not find a more convincing explanation. I have to smile at Augustine's discovery. Simplicity is so endearing in great persons.

I accept the dialectic of the church and I accept it with Hegelian fatalism. It's clear that the Holy Spirit's intervention in Vatican II has had the effect of bringing the tired old battle of a few poor, completely outnumbered stalwarts with the Pharisees into the limelight. Perhaps the Holy Spirit was thinking of Cana, when the wine was on hand in time to add renewed merriment to the general drowsiness. The council has radicalized the propheticism and Pharisaism. Pharisaism feels threatened, and is digging in its ideological heels, multiplying instruments and structures for the explanation, updating, and reinforcement of its ideology.

All religious reforms are confronted and discussed and explained from the religious experience handed down by preceding generation, rather than from rediscovering the gospel and cracking the plaster of Christian culture. The result is packed with hope and delusion. Now we have a permanent seesaw between a form of childishness and the full maturation of critical, creative consciousness. Votes are taken, meetings are held at all levels, but it is only the technique of these meetings that changes and progresses, becoming more foxy as time builds diffidence and weariness.

Renewal will spring only from a dialectical confrontation, only from a realization that Christian culture has smothered and betrayed the gospel, and that, to boot, it isn't the culture of today. It will take plenty of swings of the pickax to chop away all the crusting that covers the gospel, and it will have to be done in a hurry. But the strokes begin, and then there is fear that everything will fall to pieces; so the work is stopped. Disinterest would be the least of ills, however; what happens is that the old structures are being re-formed and streamlined. And this zeal for the modification of the old structures is called love for the church, the community, the gospel. It would be comical if the victim weren't the means of human salvation, and if macabre signs of history didn't loom to make this salvation more urgent!

We all seek spiritual renewal. From all sides comes a call for a rejuvenation of the world whose only genuine novelty is the replacement of nuclear bombs with thermonuclear bombs, the world in which certain governments commit themselves to the merely partial destruction of humanity so that we may sleep in peace, the hope being that we will be spared and others destroyed. But Christians educated in ideology defend spiritual renewal as forms of intellectual evolution—which distance them ever further from the heart of the gospel. All these reforms bear on things that ought not to be reformed, but destroyed.

Jesus really "had our number" when he said we patched old cloth with new material. Potentially important, potentially healthy forces are mobilized and institutionalized in a series of training techniques—in pedagogy, psychology, statistics—anything to make ideology acceptable. Nuns in crisis, priests tired of their old pastoral approach that fails to reach the people, are sent away to study. Maybe the approach is Socratic: we seek to reinforce what we already know is the way to the people, so we take instructions in it. And behold, we withdraw from the people, the poor.

All this bustle, this fervor, these initiatives to which the conciliar epiphany has given rise, have had the inevitable result of consolidating the church's anchorage in the bourgeois class, the ideological class. And so we search for a substitute for history. History is open and risky, impure, impious, incorrigible. History can be made only by the homeless, the roofless, the adventurous—not by lovers of closed systems, not by those who dare not risk their security. The bourgeois world has fashioned a religious poverty, and has transformed chastity into a privilege, a kind of vague, untouchable whiteness, an otherworldly superiority, an ideal where all the elegant adulteries, all the sexual creativity of our generation, find their expiatory compensation. Obedience becomes the bulwark of class privilege, where class is threatened by anarchy.

A Latin American magazine had lots of fun with the Vatican press commentary on regional Italian elections a few years ago. The Vatican press office attributed the outcome to the influence of an allegedly "leftward-drifting" secular press. As if right-wing clergy had no space and liberty to express their own position! If you're going to go with ideology, for goodness' sake be a little more modern, a little more profound!

Our houses, our lifestyle, the measuring sticks we judge our greatness and our "heroism" by—we get these all from the bourgeois class. When I was in the northeast of Argentina, I saw old persons sleeping on "beds" that made the torture-racks of the martyrs look like feather mattresses. I saw the poor on penitential fasts they didn't even know they were on. Either they simply had to, or else they did it out of love when an unexpected guest arrived just at suppertime. The poor showed me how bourgeois our lifestyle, our thinking, our preaching, our prayer is. And all that we do by way of "renewal" only roots us deeper in this world. We keep choosing this world instead of choosing the poor, and in order to have the freedom not to choose, in order not to notice, in the name of the gospel we deny class division, and we appeal to a mythical Adam emerging from the hands of God without sociological specifications.

All human beings are as equal as peas in a pod—only, the peas are called brothers and sisters. But a brotherly/sisterly communion is a relationship that we must *create,* and it is a dramatic one: it has a more and a less, a nothing, an opposition. The council ought to have concluded with a proposal to get started dismantling! But that would have been to admit that the look in Jesus' eyes had made the Pharisees ashamed of being Pharisees, and persuaded them to abandon tradition in favor of truth and justice. Could they have done that? This is the question that burns my insides and tortures me.

13

Our Trust and the Gospel's Secret

In order to arrive at admiration and co-creation, those two shining jewels of the gospel, we would have to have nothing to defend, nothing to lose. We would have come to the point at which Peter and Andrew left their nets and their father, and therefore we would have seen the Other, the Lord Jesus, passing by, instead of being involved in defending what we call our "doctrine."

It looks like a simple formula, if you can call throwing in your lot with the poor and the oppressed a formula. But what if there are no poor? Couldn't the gospel be lived in a society that eliminated every type of oppression? Must we insist that our society is unjust just so we can "practice the gospel"? Must subversives, the "asocial," the revolutionaries, find oppression, and a crowd of oppressed, in every "just" society?

Easy, easy, don't throw that stone! I'm not saying that being a Christian means being a subversive or a revolutionary. I have no intention of saying we have to decide immediately to rally 'round the banner of revolution. I'm simply trying to say that a certain degree of sensitivity, and a certain interpretative key, reveal that there are still injustices, and victims of injustice, and this means that our worldview is superficial and—once more—bourgeois. And it is superficial and bourgeois—and a position to be rejected by a follower of the gospel—to say that all the agitation about these injustices and their victims is simply the work of social misfits. "There will always be injustices and victims of injustice in society, but there will always be persons who won't feel as if they're living unless they can jump all over the established order." These are armchair diagnoses, and seem valid only in the parlor where the elite meet to think. They become unforgivable when confronted with experience.

I remember reading an old French book I found in the library of our home when I was a teenager. I remember only its title and one more thing about it. It was called *Récit d'une soeur*—"A sister's tale," and it contained the memoirs of a family of diplomats. In Brussels, during the first half of the nineteenth century, a group of European diplomats invited a group of Italian exiles to a soirée. Among the invitees were Confalonieri, Gioberti, and others. And the spiritual quality of the guests of honor, considered by Austria to be common delinquents, sealed closer ties with their hosts abroad than any political initiative could ever have managed.

How often I have recalled this reading from my youth when I've encountered "subversives." From the viewpoint of our assemblies, from the stagnant categories of our culture, these are society's enemies. But when you get up close, these enemies of society show too many signs of the gospel to refute. And if you tried to refute them, you'd know at once that you were on the side of Annas and Caiphas. Why shouldn't there be those who can see the injustice, see the martyrs for freedom, in an opulent society like that of North America, as well as see the "humiliated and the wronged" (Tolstoy) in the people's democracies like that of the Soviet Union? It's a problem of seeing. It's a problem of interior availability.

We religious, too, discover the oppressed, the suffering, the socially marginalized. It would be slanderous to say we spend all day in one continuous cocktail party. But we have never transcended the individualistic, bourgeois "benefactions and charity" formula, the formula of an acritical beneficence that rushes to the aid of persons, but closes its eyes to the historical complexity in which they live and by which they are being victimized. We're a permanent "Red Cross," bandaging bloody arms and legs, without even knowing what language is spoken by the casualty brought in on a stretcher. For centuries we've called this "universal charity." We don't want to get ourselves dirty, so we stay out of "politics," and we contribute to keeping alive in the world the miseries to which we've dedicated ourselves.

"The poor you will always have with you." This statement, taken literally, has been used as an argument—or excuse—for our options. Why look for and try to eradicate the causes of poverty if its continued presence has been guaranteed?

All the ideological defenses we use for the continuation of our practice of abstract charity would instantly collapse if we had the courage to make an option for the oppressed, throw in our lot with the oppressed, even just by way of experiment. It would have to be in full cognizance of cause. The business would be risky. It would be risky because it would place us in danger of entertaining admiration, and of engaging upon co-creation. These are not things that come mechanically, through an explosion of the laws of history. This is the naivety and the limitation of Marxism, and even Christians and wise religious can fall into its trap. The option for the poor is not simply and automatically evangelical. What is evangelical is the rejoicing of Christ because the Father has revealed to the lowly what he has hidden from the great and wise. What is evangelical is to go to illiterates with their gnarled hands and make them completely and totally responsible for the kingdom.

In our reading of the gospel, responsibility for the kingdom on the part of John and Mary Doe is transferred to privileged individuals, and to authority—to a "Who heareth you, heareth me," rather than to human trust, trust in things like poverty and lowliness, things that are despised and treated as refuse. But *this* is what is specifically evangelical. The heresy of Marxism emerges when honest, straightforward persons refuse to accept mistrust of the human being. All the "heterodox," Marxist or Protestant, are at one in their protest against a mistrust of the human being. *Trust in the human being is the secret of the gospel.* It would be hypocritical of us to think that only Marxists are guilty of this mistrust.

We Christians, we the church, fall into the same sin. Marxism speaks of cooperative management and self-management. The church speaks of collegiality, with the intuition that this concept will open up dimensions so vast that a lonely verticalism will be corrected. But this "step," this "provision," cannot be accomplished by legislation. It must come from a radical change of heart.

Political and church co-management structures can be betrayed by a heart incapable of admiration. The ecstasy of Christ before the poor as the repositories of the Father's secrets is the sign of a heart that is poor and therefore capable of loving without reserve.

Who Is a Christian?

The question has frequently been asked, in recent years, what the specific mark of the Christian is. The question is a logical one: it arises in the vacuum left by the disappearance of an erroneous division of the Christian into two parts. Christendom has disappeared, the division of the world into two parallel societies has disappeared, world history is being looked upon as one salvation history. And so it is normal that persons reared in the sacred precincts of Catholic education, but now thrust into a world without distinctions of this kind, should wonder why they are still walking around with the complication of being a Christian hanging around their necks.

This quandary has provoked an anxious search, in which anyone with a bit of a nose for psychology can discern the components of fear and self-interest: What need is there to be a Christian? No one asks what need there is to breathe or move, what decisions to make and what programs to develop today in order to breathe or move. Everyone knows that breathing and moving are simply necessary for life to go on. But we have been educated in Christianity as "content," as a special, distinct program of life—as an ideology rather than as life—and we cannot avoid our anguished wondering whether this ideology still has any credit in the world. We cannot help wondering whether, in the ongoing confluence of projects to which history invites us (but accepting or eliminating our programs without appeal), there is still any point in presenting our project. What good is it to a Christian?

Jesus would shake his head at such a question, as he shook his head at Nicodemus, a teacher in Israel: How can you not know these things? Christians are persons born from on high. They need launch no projects. They need only be reborn. The Christian, my friend, is a person with two arms and two legs, like any biped you see walking along the street. The less easily you can distinguish Christians from everyone else, the better. In fact, this is an excellent test of a Christian: that he or she be indistinguishable from anyone else. But their reborn being manifests itself in faith in the human being, faith on the level where the human being is naked, poor, and defenseless, above and beyond economic, intellectual, or esthetic values, the elements that stimulate our interest and our various appetites.

And this faith in the human being is not the fruit of an act of the will, or a "tactic" or strategy for making use of one's neighbor. It is the consequence of a conversion. It is a global, unitary discovery. It is a refraction of that unique relationship with God called divine faith. It is, as it were, an aspect of this new way of looking at life as something essential, as something important and beautiful in itself, independently of the role one may have in it, independently of the part one plays. It is a new feeling of being alive, because life is rooted in a deep love from which you cannot release yourself even if you struggle to pry yourself away. Life acquires a quality of the definitive, of the interesting. Life wins a weight all its own, heretofore unknown.

This discovery awakens alternate surges of anguish and deep joy, and this is why contemplatives (I know I'm repeating myself: those with the rare privilege of looking on life bare, looking on it with, I would say, no other motivation than simply the will to see it as it is) are touched at the most sensitive points of pain and joy. Jesus exulted at the sight of the flowers and grass of the field on a spring morning, and admired the phenomenon of the light of true and essential wisdom he beheld in the eyes of a shack-dweller of his time. And he confided to his friends his sadness when the human incapacity to see had handed him over to be crucified.

This confidence in the human being, this taste for the person, does not spring up spontaneously in political struggle, even if battle is seen and joined on the side of the people, the side of oppressed. And when the assault troops who have been used to bring down the tyrant are sent home, it is discovered that the passion for justice, the heroic assault to set unjust relations on their ear, is not always motivated by faith in the human being, which is another way of saying "friendship," another way of expressing a relationship purged of selfishness. This trust cannot live on the platonic plane of intentions. It can live only on the level of practice— or, if we aren't afraid of the word, "praxis." Garaudy's "self-management" rings of something richer than economic decisions. It is an economic and political "explicitation" of this confidence in the human being. We must become accustomed to living the "events of the Spirit" in historical and political decisions, and this is where we are unprepared.

The ideologues have created armchair "Christian virtues," artificial events of the Spirit, a kind of Christian morning gymnastics.

It reminds you of the bourgeois who does fifty laps around his yard in the morning because that's the last time he'll move a muscle till the next morning. For the shantytown worker of Buenos Aires or Mexico City, "exercise" means walking five or six hours a day to get to work and back. We're even bourgeois in our virtue. We've taught ourselves to take our walks in walled-in yards. Riding a bicycle means sitting indoors on a gymnastic device labeled "Made in USA." We move, but we don't budge. We lift heavy objects, not to put them in a more convenient place, but to "keep in shape." And we can speak of poverty without speaking of the poor.

Years ago I caused a sensation with an article I wouldn't publish today—I'm no longer that frank—entitled, "Prepararsi all 'amore"—Get Ready for Love." I suggested to teenagers certain motivations for continency by way of preparing for a future relationship. An educator told me that the very title was scandalous. Today I understand the objection: chastity, like poverty, is viewed idealistically. Within the monastic enclosure, poverty and chastity are realities with body and value in themselves. It isn't a matter of the relationship of the Christian with the poor, or of a man with a woman. It is a gazing upon Lady Poverty, or Lady Chastity, and with this idealization we have the opportunity to mold the two "ladies" to our own taste.

Many religious find it all but impossible to recognize the virtues, the supernatural endowments, of certain decisions, attitudes, or relationships that have the lowliness of ordinary acts continually performed by simple mortals. A walk in the monastery garden doesn't get your feet sweaty. Running down a side road out in the country to catch the 6 A.M. bus, and running out of the factory gate to catch another to ride home, gets your feet dirty. This is hard reality, and scarcely consonant with good character or special behavior, we of the religious life feel.

There's no virtue called "trust in the human being." I can't take fifty deep breaths a morning and say as I inhale, "I believe," and then as I exhale, "in the human being." Faith in the human being is a renewed relationship. It's the sign of the inner rebirth offered Nicodemus by Jesus as the only solution. O Israelite, O Pharisee, O new person! Yes, Nicodemus, it's like reentering your mother's womb and beginning life with different eyes, with a new heart, with new senses. It's being you and not-you. There are remarks in the gospel that make my heart leap. Isn't this the carpenter's son? Aren't his parents our neighbors? What is this "unusual" thing about him? How comes it that he isn't like others and is like others?

Christ inaugurates the Christian mystery that we seek ever to refuse—living idealistically as we do, with our Christian being on the one side and our being-in-the-world on the other. Is this due to our Western Christian culture? Should we lay it all to the account of Greek idealism? Or is it merely a ploy of our ego to get out of a lot of work and make room for the super-I in this self-splitting of ours? It is very difficult to watch the supernatural virtues disappear in the gray waters of daily reality. Psychic health in a Christian context manifests itself as a rejection of the super-I, in a will to be like everyone else. It means not refusing any human task, especially the harder and less glorious ones.

Conversion of Heart

When being human escapes the plane of the super-I, escapes the shame of having ascended to this false sublimity, it's understandable that there should be vibrations confusing the super-I with an active, dynamic presence of the Spirit, because the presence of the Spirit radically alters our way of regarding other persons, things, and time. But it hurts, really hurts, to think that our education, coarse because unrealistically exalted, makes us scowl at this "reduction" of being-Christian, this trust in the human being, which is synonymous with friendship. Here we have a friendship that spreads out to include both human beings and things. Just think of Saint Francis and we can dispense with long explanations. But this is the true test of "operation rebirth."

To me, the Christian is someone capable of three miracles: the ones described in the sixth chapter of Saint Matthew and the tenth chapter of Saint Luke. See the lilies of the field. Gaze at them, feast your eyes. Use your eyes to search out the beauty of God resplendent in the flower of this moment, at the peak of its vitality. Turn your ear to the language of God, and discover the true meaning of simple things in the lives of simple persons. Feel the love the Father has for us in the beauty he has spread before our eyes, and the beauty he has spread before us in the acceptance of friendship.

The starting point for the journey to this goal is the rejection of the super-I, the rejection of the hieratic intangibility that has even been the aim of Christian education. But it would be false to feel ourselves to be authentic Christians just because we'd doffed the martian costume of the priest to don the suit of the bourgeois businessman. The super-I is adaptable to all changes of garb, even the most abject. The crucial thing for the super-I is to live on a level where there is no life. It will not even do any good to put on the worker's overalls. Conversion of heart is the sole condition.

We must be on the alert. The counterfeiters are always busy. When I was a teenager, the Christian was somebody pious, and we filled galleries with men and women rolling their eyes heavenward with otherworldly looks on their faces. Now the fashion is the ordinary person, the man on the street, the stroller who spits and belches, and is ill clothed. The attraction for the rustic life and simple companionship, the nostalgia for good sense after the intoxication of logic, the lure of estheticism—all these are but bourgeois or popular translations of the person reborn in the Spirit.

Jesus didn't go out among fisher folk to be bored by the ramblings of theologians and doctors, but out of sym-pathy (how I wish this word could recover its original meaning!) for simple persons. Jesus entrusted his project to them completely. He accepted the fact that human vacillation, ambiguity, and inconsistency would make the project of the kingdom a thing most fragile. On the other hand, he does not admire those who consider themselves fortunate, spared the hard labor of thought, the pure of mind, out on the frontiers of speculation. Jesus doesn't say: "Blessed are you the pure, the genuine, the authentic; and woe to us who must shoulder the burden of thinking for you as well." His is not an idealistic, bourgeois admiration. It is an admiration that moves from the proclamation of his program to co-management and self-management. I hope that the theologians—a fastidious sort, you know!—will permit me this bit of humor. The three admirations in an idealistic key are a help to the bourgeois world in reinforcing its distance and postponing the advent of friendship.

Jesus' admiration translates into a sym-pathetic lifestyle of intimate association. Here was a life tormented by incomprehension, doubts, jealousies—by all the peaks and valleys of our threadbare existence. This admiration seems contradicted by bitter expressions, by moments ringing with disappointment. "You of little faith, I know not of what spirit you are! Get behind me, Satan! Why did you doubt?" But the admiration surges anew as God's commitment, as a covenant that women and men can allow themselves to betray but which for God is indestructible. We cannot offer this confidence, for we have no control over the instability of others, over their terrible changes of state, over the inconsistencies so familiar to us from personal experience. But this is the road to friendship.

Today, the Holy Spirit has asked a service of the church, in this age of a crisis of communion. The Holy Spirit has asked the church to bestow on the world the gift of friendship. Our age is one of a crisis of communion in the sense that the desire for communion has become acute, whereas the possibility of communion seems a dim and distant prospect. It may be that these are but two aspects of the same problem. As the demand for communion sharpens, the difficulties begin to be seen from "close up," and they look bigger than before.

I'm convinced that this path and this path alone is the way to faith in Christ today. Human beings, powerful in so many ways, discover their essential impotence in the sole enterprise that is crucial, in the true criterion of a successful life: relationship, communication. I see no other way of presenting Christ to today's generation in its culture crisis than to present him as "the other" and present him in others.

All the fears of those in charge of orthodoxy cannot alter the world's cultural state, its capacity for receiving truth—just as they cannot change the nature of the engagement, the quality of the covenant, that God renews with women and men in every age. This calls for the urgent, serious conversion of Christians who have the interests of the kingdom at heart and feel a responsibility for evangelization.

The time has come for a movement from the level of an idealistic faith to the rediscovery of the Absolute Other, rendered visible and brought near in the presence of nonabsolute others, as the eternal beauty of the Father is spread before our eyes in the beauty of flowers of the field, so soon to fall and be cast in the fire.

The Holy Spirit has asked this of the church, it seems to me, not for the reinforcement of its ideological power by means of everything that progress has discovered that can be used to make an ideology more palatable and thereby less liberating. The Holy Spirit asks much less of us than that we should busy ourselves like little bees, buzzing about day and night tirelessly, around a hive that has no honey. He asks us for less money, less movement, fewer planeloads of nuns and priests and prelates everlastingly crossing the ocean. The Spirit does not need so many crisis specialists from Spain to go to Chile, from France to go to Haiti. The Spirit asks much less, but something far more difficult.

The essential thing, the simple thing, has always been more difficult, the last thing to be understood. The human way leads not from the simple to the complicated, but from the complicated to the simple. Simplicity calls for extraordinary courage: the courage to accept criticism. This could not have been asked of every sector of the church. But apparently it could and should be asked of those in a "state of perfection," those committed to a "full time" service of the Holy Spirit. These persons have been looking for something specific to distinguish them from simple Christians. Well, this shall be a sign: a virgin shall bear God-with-us, Emmanuel, the Friend, the one who identifies totally with the poor, the lower class, where it is commonly thought that not a single ray of wisdom penetrates, where one looks for an arm for lifting, and a back for bending over the soil, but not for projects of the world salvation. No, certainly not there!

I don't mean the church should consist of illiterates, or that evangelization demands the a priori rejection of what technology places at our disposal for coming to know ideas and spreading them effectively. After all, sharing with the poor, defending their dignity and their justice, which Jesus so admires, are necessary means. Marginalization, inferiority, perpetual victimization by violence, aren't an ideal. Violence is an evil, and sin is not to be willed in order that the wisdom of God may shine in all its splendor. This would be a "diametrical contradiction," as the young say.

Evangelizing means proclaiming and creating liberation from sin and hence from all forms of slavery. This liberation, this passage from a relationship of slavery to a relationship of communion, necessarily involves passing by way of an ideology. It means making use of certain elements of technology and forms of organization that cannot be the result of improvisation. Long reflection and patient study are necessary. I don't deny the role of intelligence, instruction, technology. The Christian must use these just as any human being on earth must, without timidity, accepting the moral risk, accepting the doubt, involved. Each man and woman must accept the doubt as to whether this choice will be completely positive, or instead will cause their whole moral structure to creak from top to bottom.

When I refer to admiration and co-creation as evangelical values I'm speaking of an attitude of love, liberty, and respect that is of course reflected in outward choices and evaluations, reflected in one's way of looking at life and hence of using means to change the world and human relationships. I make no distinction between a Christian and another human being, all reflecting on their work in the world.

14

The Poor Must Build
Their Church

A religious group asked me what "distinguishes" them—
whether there is anything special about them vis-à-vis other persons. I think a religious group has the particular task of making the
church visible. A religious group has the specific task of *anticipat-
ing* an image of the church, and so I see it as a community marked
by three visible signs: freedom, love, and joy.

I don't care for making distinctions between religious (under the
vows of a religious congregation) and other Christians. I think that
life and time will cancel the distinctions between them, and make
perfectly clear what is substantial for a religious group.

Today in Latin America there is only one choice: to be church, to
transfer the emphasis from creating church to being church. I see
this as something most urgent in Latin America. To me, freedom is
capsulized in the ability to admire and to collaborate, to co-create
with persons outside the categories of admiration and collaboration adopted by politicians, entrepreneurs, and the middle class.
For this it will be absolutely necessary to share the life of the poor. It
is absurd to think in categories of equality and communion when
our way of living, our lifestyle, is already established as a relationship of teacher to pupil, when we are rulers, heads, and directors.
The celebrated "poverty of spirit," in which the spirit sashays
blissfully along while the body stays somewhere else, can be conceived only in an idealistic framework. And I tell my colleagues:

"Don't you think this act's been on the program long enough. The battle we have to win, the step we have to take, is to build a poor, proletarian, popular church, and this will not occur as long as we reason in dualistic categories of soul and body, of poor spirit and rich existence. If you don't feel like it, change vocations. Tell our Lord honestly you'd rather change occupations."

I think more damage is done to the interests of the kingdom of God today by those who reduce everything to a Christian ideology than by opponents and atheists. And so I think the kind of response we tend to give to the initiatives of Vatican II only postpones the time we forecast by it. The Holy Spirit points one way, and we march off in the opposite direction. It may be that this counter-march, reinforcing the ideological line, will make the need for a response so urgent—a response consisting in praxis, and making common cause and a common life with our opponents—that it will actually balance out on the plus side, and actually foster the renewal proclaimed by the council.

I know, I know—a reduction of the Christian conversion to this capacity for admiration and co-creation will be distasteful to a great many persons. Ideologues will find it abstract and poetic, and hence of no use to a world becoming daily more aware of a need for salvation. It will be called dallying with poetry. On the other hand, it will seem spiritualistic to those incapable of conceiving liberation in any but political terms. I can't escape these interpretive criticisms once I decide to conduct my discourse on ideological grounds.

Just today, as I'm writing this, I received a letter from a group of Latin American administrators who, after having worked so long in the decision-making echelon, decided to leave their jobs and go to work at the grassroots. I've spoken so much of the grassroots, the "base," that I may surely be excused from giving a definition. And I shall be forgiven for not identifying this particular group more closely, for many reasons. But I've kept the letter, lest I be accused of inventing it! Here is an extract:

Contact with the world of the country folk, and especially with destitution, and a simple life for ourselves, has been so great a blessing that were it not for the . . . [let's call them the Brothers of the Five Wounds] with their *countertestimony*, and the loneliness of our pastoral life, our cup would be full.

In sum: we continue our journey along our chosen route, and
there are interesting signs, which would seem to come from
our Friend, but the recipe will be not to get too smug, but to
draw conclusions, and keep drawing conclusions, from our
activity, through a dialectical analysis of praxis, and the
continual listening, listening, listening to the people, and then
listening, listening to the unostentatious—to those who can
speak a word that will fill us with life, because that's where
God is and it's God who speaks out and cries out, trying to
launch the real history of the love that is asked of us and that
costs us so much because it means loving others as ourselves.

My friend apologizes later in the letter for being an administrator
and "not much of a writer." And of course his words are neither
enigmatic nor poetic, because they come from the concrete experience of someone in tune with the people.

If only all priests and religious would agree that they can't think
like the people when they look at the people from the outside—that
they can't think like the poor when they live like the rich—they
would understand everything. They would understand that "admiration" is so dynamic and so revolutionary a word in a gospel
context that it outstrips anything any Lenin on earth could have
discovered. But what sign of liberty can emerge from a community
living entirely outside a context of liberation? The experience of
this group of administrators has demolished, in practice, so many
of the defenses with which we hide our unwillingness to make a
choice: "You will never be entirely as they. You cannot live on their
actual level. Should Christians be ignorant? Should evangelization
exclude all kinds of training, and promote only Franciscan simplicity?" These difficulties come up in every meeting, and immediately
betray those who are averse to any descent to the level of praxis.
Why should they step down from their peaceful, ideological tower
and disappear, making an option like that of the administrators
who had had secure and enviable careers?

That "listen, listen, listen" is not something I put in the letter to
make my polemical point. It's literally what was in the letter. And
this is the "admiration" I'm talking about. These administrators
come out of a planning structure. One day they noticed that human
beings were a cipher in their calculations, and they decided to make

friends with the cipher. They didn't abandon their work, their training, they merely demolished the wall separating them from these friends. As Christians they made a choice. That choice changed little of their professional activity on the surface. But the change was an essential one. They moved from management to co-management, from deciding for others to sharing. That is, instead of continuing in work that would shore up the forces of oppression, they devoted themselves to a liberation task. They moved from diffidence in the human being ("country folk don't think; we have to think for them") to confidence ("let's think with them"). In this collaboration, this co-creation, we contribute the techniques, and they contribute the wisdom.

Listen, Listen, Listen

The church will be able to change only on one condition: that it become a church of the poor. In this renewal, we the Pharisees, who cannot belong to the simple folk to whom "the affairs of God" are revealed, can at least enter among them with admiration and co-creation. Just as we cannot be lilies of the field and birds of the air, where God manifests the divine beauty and solicitude for the particulars of creation, and shows us all the motions of a tender, delicate heart—so neither can we be the simple folk. We know about theology. The life we lead was an idea, a program, first. That is, we have had the time and freedom to think.

We are not poor because we were born poor, as one is born to achieve a certain height and weight. We have gotten together and discussed poverty, and then decided to have some. So we honed it down, planed it, "adapted" it, and finally let it into the house.

One day a brother asked me, "Should I put on my regular pants or my witness pants?" He meant it as a joke, but it's a good deal more serious than it sounds. We should start out by admitting, without despair and without scandalizing ourselves, that we are the Pharisees—the ones who transport the past, with all its laws and traditions.

Saint Paul is not ashamed to say that he was a Pharisee, burning with love for the law, meticulously observant. This is not a superfluous detail for us. Our own conversion will bear the mark of a like past. All religious meetings bear on the reform of Pharisaism—

on lightening the burden of the Pharisaic tradition. And so they design an image of the reformed Pharisee, a more agile, more acceptable image—and therefore ever more convinced that "I am not like the rest."

Translated into the language of religious who are trying to camouflage their Pharisaical origin, this will read: "We go among the poor not to teach, but to learn." This is false. It misses the point. Our "descent" to the poor to terms of "teaching" and "learning" is immediately suspect. It isn't true, because if instruction is the criterion, then I'm much more the instructor than the country folk of Bojó and much more than Pedro who lived with me. I have material for discourse with them ad infinitum. Often in our conversations they get "jammed." After a few words about the rain, the sun, the cold or heat, they wouldn't know what to say if I didn't "cue" them; and we talk about my interests. Otherwise the talk would be about their life, which they intuit with an infallible intuition.

No, I haven't come to learn a thing. And I'm not about to renounce knowledge that the years have given me and that I've tried to cultivate as a gift of God. The administrator whose letter I quoted went back to town to pick up books and tools, because his new life had placed him before practical difficulties that were not encompassed by his expertise. This isn't the way to work. This is the way not to work. When Saint Paul speaks of a fanatical Pharisaism, he doesn't say he's "reformed." He says:

> Those things I used to consider gain I have now reappraised as loss in the light of Christ. . . . I have accounted all else rubbish so that Christ may be my wealth and I may be in him, *not having any justice of my own based on observance of the law.* The justice I possess is that which comes through faith in Christ [Phil. 3:7–9].

All our thinking, so long as it is rooted in laws, is still essentially Pharisaical. Saint Paul is not an unlettered person. His evangelization is certainly not the simple, direct message the gospel gives us. We feel ourselves to be in the presence of a person who has studied, and who "knows." We feel a message not sown in virgin soil, but in a soil rich with the cultural values of its time. But this does not deprive Paul of his life of faith, of his simple regard of faith, on which all his anthropology and christology is based. The whole dissertation of the Letter to the Romans demonstrates that the Lord Jesus has demolished the logic demanded by the Greeks, to found salvation on faith alone.

Among the poor and with the poor, on the side God has chosen as the place of revelation, we religious can stand neither as teachers, nor as disciples, nor as those who guide, nor as those who serve. We can stand here only with admiration. *Listen, listen, listen.* This is our true conversion. Paul after his conversion is neither Peter nor Andrew nor any of the fisher folk of Miletus who embrace him on the shore in despair at his departure. He knows that it is not his lucubrations that will save him and others, but Christ Jesus. And so he goes in search of Christ Jesus, in the place where he reveals himself, in the place where he has promised to manifest himself.

And we poor religious are so profoundly stricken with Pharisaism, so deformed by our professionalism, that when I propose these notions in a religious group the response is: "So the poor are perfect, then? Have they no sin, as the rich and the mighty have?" These questions do very well as a test. The questioners have not been converted. They reason in Pharisaical categories. I feel like shaking the dust from my feet and moving on. "The kingdom of God shall be taken away from you and given to a nation that will yield a rich harvest" (Matt. 21:43).

Then I reflect that these religious are my brothers and sisters, who have received a warped professional training. If we could have a schematic division in the church between employers and employees, as in a factory, religious could recover a great deal for wrongful injury, as their poor professional training is truly profound, and seemingly without remedy. Superiors should think about this seriously before making decisions that only reinforce distortions.

However, I think that religious groups are full of good will. And I think—last, but not least—that in seeking their liberation, I find my own. Are the poor the only sinners? Who are unhappier, the big investors, the rich—or simple folk? I have no intention of repeating the infallible pronouncements I've heard in religious circles on the simple life, the goodness of the poor—or, on the contrary, on their vices! Our ability to beat around the bush is astounding. We'll do anything to avoid a response that each of us will feel in our heart as urgent and unpostponable.

Our philosophical education furnishes us with truly dangerous weapons. In religious gatherings we find all the bourgeois clichés, the bourgeois manner of viewing the world, the bourgeois appraisal of the poor and situations of poverty, and we find them done to a turn and served up in a syrup of risk-free charity.

A few observations and questions will suffice to make it crystal clear in what world and on what level the religious life has remained entangled. When we state that the religious life is a "life of the people," we are lying, and we ought to begin to admit it. Such honesty will carry us to the conclusion that we can't think with the people and as the people while remaining anchored to the bourgeois class. If you want to know what the bourgeois read, what newspapers are published in a country, what magazines there are (except pornography) for the bourgeois—all you have to do is glance at the table or the magazine rack in a monastery or convent parlor.

A philosophy of praxis, notwithstanding all its errors, which we should admit, has the merit of "recomposing" human beings, putting them back together in the unity in which their creator made them. And it has made this important discovery: human beings *are, think, and act* in a more profound unity than they themselves imagine. Inconsistencies are possible and real, but the inconsistencies are deviations, and never foster a positive, creative synthesis. Inconsistencies decidedly weaken our capacity to create. They are not symptoms of health. They are pathological, evidently. That a person should be rich and act as a poor person can happen, but only in a schizophrenic.

Make Your Own Church

Who are the poor, who are the oppressed? The question drags from chapter room to chapter room and meeting to meeting. My friends the administrators found them without much looking. They are not some rare species, like some of the animals of our mountains. They haven't held endless congresses and meetings to draw up a list of qualifications for candidacy. One breach they have made, yes—a decisive, violent, painful separation, and not without hesitation, not without opinions and intervention on the part of relatives, friends, and spiritual advisors: "What are you doing? Leaping off a cliff? You're abandoning your security for insecurity? You know what you're leaving, and you don't know what you're getting into. And the children!"

Ah, yes, the children. The bourgeois family has always imagined it was sacrificing for its children, and accepting an intolerably hard life of work, "for the children"! How often I've heard this language on the lips of "knights of industry"! "I'm willing to live on a crust of bread a day, sleep on a mat on the ground! For that matter, I come from a poor family. My children oblige me to this dog's life. I'm doing it for them!" (Then they serenely immolate their children in various wars of East and West or drive them to drugs by their stubborn defense of prestige and status.)

The administrators hesitated as any normal person would, in the face of a risk, a leap. This is an encounter with the cowardice lurking within each of us. This is reckoning with our own weakness. Nobody's born with a lion's heart. But in their hesitations, their period of wonderings, "Do we or don't we?," they never included theoretical considerations. They never included our long dissertations. "How will we get in, how are we going to imitate them, what kind of trousers should we take with us?"

Religious have no sense of breach, of conversion, of a leap in the dark. We are what we are already, we're there already, we've always been there. The last hidebound defense (I've come to know all the questions and defenses by heart) in religious assemblies is: "But isn't this what we've always done? Isn't this what we've always taught?" This is why Jesus doesn't propose things for Nicodemus to do. He'd have stumbled right into the response of the rich: "This I've always done." He proposes that he be reborn, that he become new.

The challenge to the adminstrators was not to work *in the favor of the poor.* They were already doing this, and very effectively, I can guarantee you. But what happened was that their work didn't actually operate in favor of the poor. It served only to enrich the rich and empower the powerful. It wasn't their work they had to change. It was their relationship with nonpossessors. That called for a conversion and revolution in their state of life.

Their change of state didn't interfere with their reflection. Quite the contrary. Only, their reflection is not on how and where to be "inserted." Their reflection begins with insertion and admiration, with listening, listening, listening, because they didn't go out to enhance their status as administrators, they went out to clarify their activity and thereby deliver themselves from frustration, deliver themselves from the onus of actually undoing liberation.

The way religious discover the poor, or go to the poor, is so often vitiated in its point of departure. It fails to begin with a conversion—with the certain conviction that life in a certain milieu is sterile, that the gospel, which is liberation, becomes a dead letter in this milieu, for the gospel is liberation only if it emerges in a communion of sisters and brothers, and such a communion arises only from the sincerity of admiration: "I praise you, Father. . . . "

For the church actually to experience a total conversion, there would have to be, after the shining light of the conciliar call for a church of the poor, the emergence of this call in a decision: the poor must make their church! It is not we Pharisees who must build the church of the poor. This is the true, the only revolution, the one awaited by so many within the church, however implicitly—by so many who feel themselves outside and against the church. Once the council was over we should have said to ourselves: "Now our part is finished. Let's wait for the poor to do their part." A decision like that would have had greater repercussions than the Copernican revolution.

The will of the Holy Spirit—a church of the poor—seems to me to be not so much an invitation to today's hierarchy to become poor (although such an invitation would not be superfluous), as the blossoming in the church of an awareness of not being on the level of the poor, of being on the side of injustice rather than pointing an accusatory finger at injustice and the unjust. It was an invitation to the poor rather than an admonishment of the rich. It was a call to the poor: make your own church.

The error of the Pharisees, the irremediable paralysis of Pharisaism, is this: believing that God's only sanctuary, the only assembly in which God speaks, God's consultative, deliberative, and executive assembly, is where they themselves sit. We hear of catholicity, of ecumenism, of universality, of a Christ not of Christians alone but transcending all ages and all parishes, the deliverer of Muslim and Buddhist and communist and anarchist as well as of the practicing Catholic and the little old woman who goes to Mass every day. But de facto this "universality" is always interpreted in the style of Rome, which graciously extends the rights of citizenship to subject peoples who have demonstrated their zeal for the law, especially in the paying of taxes.

"Church of the poor" really means that the poor are to build their own church. We must never tire of repeating this. What we Pharisees can do that will be most useful for the church will be to listen, listen, listen. This is a practical translation of the contemplative attitude that made Jesus leap for joy at the wisdom of his Father. We Pharisees, too, can and must find our way of littleness and childhood, because it's the only way to the kingdom of heaven. We must break off the search for our isolation and enter into the blessedness of the poor and the little, abandoning the conviction that we are "all things and everyone," and finding trust in simple folk. Trust is possible only in praxis, in a common quest for liberation. If we freeze it in a council chamber, it is at once transformed into an idea, and thereby becomes controvertible, attackable, subject to criticism.

We play with ideas as a boxer plays with his punching bag, for training. It's time we realized that this game is fruitless. All ought to open their eyes—those who leave us in the sterility of our existential situation, and those who, to be fruitful, must leave the church. A Mexican friend of mine told me: "Out of fidelity to Christ, I became an atheist, and I certainly didn't need any theological games to recover my faith, in this 'death of God' society." Our idealistic warping resists even this message sent us by the Spirit, through the desertions, the weariness, the anemia we see threatening the religious life. And the defense is that the "deserters" needed a pretext for their emotional immaturity, or their psychological or spiritual weakness. If our groupings, our structures are calculated to support an immature man or woman for years, especially if it is to be for many years, then our structures are incubators, not nuclei for the making of history.

Could not much of this "emotional immaturity" have matured in "historical" involvement, in a real struggle for liberation? Would not a confrontation with the real world, the interest at work in a life spent for something worthwhile—something that puts us in the same basket with those who are the most altruistic and most seriously active in the making of history—would not a life like this have the function of making us emotionally more mature? The prevailing official diagnosis, which dismisses all crises with a wave of the hand, and which is intended to defend the honor and the future of the de facto religious institution, as well as to protect from discouragement those who remain, looks to me like a boomerang, which will turn back on those who use it as a defensive weapon.

I know that my arguments will not chip away the rock that shattered the humanity of Christ. But an appeal to Christ, to his death and resurrection, will cause us to regard this rock not in terms of an epilogue to death, but a prologue to resurrection. And this will give us hope without limit.

The maturation of decision-making since the end of Vatican II shows us that the formula, "Go to the poor"—the formula that calls for a shift of the center of gravity from the boarding schools to the slums and shacks, from the religious houses with a swimming pool and watered gardens to a quarter where drinking water is scarce—is no magic formula. As always, theorized in idealistic, ideological categories, it is a dangerous formula. The ideology of the poor is the Marxist ideology, make no mistake. At the tip of the iceberg, this ideology is free of, or is becoming free of, any necessary implication of atheism. Garaudy says, "Atheism is not the necessary basis for revolutionary action." But Garaudy is a "heretic," and it will be years before heresy will penetrate praxis. These prophetic intuitions are reliable, but they are sporadic anticipations, and it will be some time before history will accept them and assimilate them.

On the surface, Protestants and Catholics come to blows no longer. But beneath the surface the honeymoon is neither constant nor universal. From their steeples, Catholics still gaze out on Protestant meetings with a jaundiced eye, and Protestant assemblies still hurl darts at the church of Rome.

An ideology of the poor must take account of a piety lived as the only escape from oppression, injustice, and enforced silence. For the moment, the shift of religious to the world of the poor has generally entailed a laicization akin to atheism, and, worse, so deep and radical an alienation that all motives for love, for self-donation, are lost, and one's very reason for being in the world becomes questionable. This is a moment requiring enormous courage on the part of those responsible for religious groups: the courage to take risks even with our faith. I believe that serenity, peace, patience, and the ability to suffer and to wait would often make these unavoidable dark nights meaningful for those who come from an "ideological," bourgeois world accustomed to encountering only ideology, and unprepared for any practical translation into praxis of the notions of friendship and collaboration.

Who Will Give the Church a New Face?

It would be absurd, or superstitious, to think that those who for years, if not for centuries, have been trained to sing in an ideological key, trained to see the poor through the concept of poverty, would suddenly be able to sing in a prophetic key. Those who for long years have been within the well-protected walls of precaution, cannot go to the banks of the Jordan to gather around an emaciated John crying in the wilderness. It is not his physical nakedness, or his daily fare, that revolts them, but his ideological nakedness. He preaches emptying; leveling hills and filling in valleys—the abolition of superiority/inferiority relationships. He seems to be preaching negativity, nihilism; speaking of himself, he proclaims that his ideal is to diminish, to disappear. He is only a voice. He is not a reformer of the Pharisaic doctrine; he is a weather vane moved by a current of fresh air that is to blow away the dust of an old, decrepit world. He is a beginning "from without." He is not a stranger to the kingdom, but he is outside it. His is not a reform, but a revolution.

And I think that the Council issued a demand not for a reform, but for a revolution. We should be convinced that we shall not be the ones to give the church a new face—to give it the capacity for an impact on history, make it leaven, salt, light, communion, and therefore true freedom. For freedom is the ability to live together and co-create. We shall not be the ones. It will be the lowly. It will not be those who are vitiated by the habit of immediately translating into an ideology what is essentially a manner of living.

It is easy to understand the concern of hierarchs over "popular experiences" or "democratizations." After all, to make a long story short, it is not "prophets," but ideologues who go among the poor. And ideologues will either be fiercely anti-Marxist (or better, against any form of "leftism"), or leftist extremists—"more Catholic than the pope." For hierarchs, the ideal solution would lie in the golden mean: the Christianity of European social democratic politicians—which would be like jumping from the frying pan into the fire. If they were to come to understand that John the Baptist revolted against the kingdom because he was of the kingdom, it would be a step forward.

The ideology of the people is an ideology of the "left." One thing is sure: it is not capitalism or laissez-faire liberalism that will stir up the people. And those who walk with the people cannot remain strangers to liberation or, therefore, to an ideology of liberation. But the Christian's involvement must be prophetic, and this is the only contribution the world expects from Christians, especially from religious. There, lost amid those who have never had a voice in the church, we shall find our manner of being Christian, and of being "religious," in the attitude of admiration of which I have spoken, which lubricates our training and our human capacities.

It is not—let me repeat, lest there be any misunderstanding—a matter of a mechanical dismantling along economic lines. For years we have ridiculed the revolutionary utopia, saying that the world would gain nothing by reversing roles and setting the poor in place of the rich. And now we say: "What is to be gained by putting the ignorant in charge of everything and proclaiming them wise?" Such mechanical interpretation of the meaning of the Christian revolution that is under way, and irreversible, is tantamount to attributing to incarnate wisdom a childish stupidity.

Jesus meant what all the most hardened conservatives repeat (though they with a warped intention): revolution begins with a change of heart, begins with inner conversion. But if you put this into a computer, and postpone the revolution till the day when all men and women will be "converted in their hearts," you turn the whole thing into a joke. A trust in human beings like Jesus' trust— the trust that the poor have spontaneously because all they have to do is touch their neighbor's hand to feel its warmth—is the fruit of a true conversion, when we have it, and the sign of contemplation. Contemplation comes by way of the dark night, by way of the complete loss of trust in self, in one's own ability, in one's own toil.

The dark night is not that narcissistic nightmare, that repeated dive into the dark well where our ego has fallen without any hope of escape. The dark night of my administrative friends came when they began to doubt that they were doing effective things. In other words, are we working for oppression or for liberation? Are we working for a more just and more humane world, or are we collaborating with division, war, hatred, and everything that, intentionally and verbally, we battle with all our might? Our relationship with God is reducible to one question, which a lay person will ask without so many nuances and academic distinctions: Are we near God or far away? Is God absent or present? Am I walking the road of light, or am I walking through the valley of death? Everything hangs on that question.

Lay persons, and especially technical professionals, are in a position to choose relationships that escape us religious, or at least that we know we don't see: the relationship between purely "technological" work and oppression, the connection between a seemingly just wage in remuneration for services rendered, and a corrupt intention on the part of those who utilize research and technology for their own profit. In comparison with their analyses, we're superficial, like the old Roman emperor who claimed he'd sniffed the tribute he'd received by way of the sewer and had noticed no stench.

If we have the courage to ask ourselves whether we are working for peace or war, we feel plunged in such deep, total anguish that we can come to wish we could simply renounce our humanity. A Venezuelan deputy, during the debates over the nationalization of oil, thought up a real bombshell to toss at the national assembly. He made some calculations and announced that every speech by a deputy cost the country 200 million bolivars. The dark night begins when one realizes that one's delay costs the world more hunger, more prostitution, more oppression, more injustice, less communion. Engineers don't know about our syllogisms. Philosophy is of no help to them with its magical capacity for dualism: intention and execution, soul and body, poverty and the poor, the poor of Yahweh and the poor of Gordiani or Carapita, word and deed.

I know the leader of a Christian movement who gives talks on *Humanae Vitae* and holds stock in a company that manufactures contraceptives. Now, there's somebody who really knows how to handle dualism. My administrator friends do not have such resources, and they must face crises of conscience "defenseless." To save themselves they switched ball parks. Obviously the dark night is a personal problem, an "ego" problem, inasmuch as it entails the loss of all one's possible relationships, a loss of identity. Rebirth, finding oneself again, can only be a rediscovery, a forging of new relationships. It cannot, then, emerge from the explanation of an idea.

This new vision, which comes to us from brothers and sisters, impinges directly on the concept of the contemplative life, which we have always seen as uprooted from existential reality. We have always regarded contemplation as an intellectual activity—with certain consequences in practical life, to be sure, but not as germinating in corporeal, material, historical situations. The contemplative has always been viewed as one delivered from all historical and political involvements. The economic structure in which we live, and in which the contemplative lives, fosters slavery or liberation, hate or love, peace or war. There are no other alternatives.

15

The Way of the Samaritan

By no manner of means do I conclude that all of us whom Jesus invites—"Come after me"—have the same role. I'm not saying that the age of the contemplatives is over, and that we must all decide to have a revolution. But all whom Jesus calls are called to one thing alone: to discover a relationship with our Father by building a communion of brothers and sisters, to bring it about in some way or other that human relationships change. "I was hungry and you gave me food": Here is the whole meaning of our life, and it is addressed to hermits and missionaries alike, to the married and the single, to all. This judgment about our life isn't a law from a legal code written twenty centuries ago. It's intrinsic to human history. It is not a law at all, it is a relationship, and it defines our encounter with our fellow men and women, our comrades in history, the people of an age, of a country. It summons us not to the mechanical observance of a law, but to a reconceptualization and a re-creation of human encounters. If my observance of "Give me to eat" leaves intact the distance between myself who eat well and my sister or brother who is hungry, then my "charity" is a mockery of both God and my sister or brother.

Social criticism reproaches Christian "charity" on this score. And there is a good deal of truth in it. Our betrayal of the gospel is such that we have failed sufficiently to reflect that Christ's interest is not so much that of getting the hungry something to eat as it is of taking a diabolical relationship and making a love relationship of it. Here the diabolical relationship is presented, is historicized, in the difference between me with a full stomach and clogged liver and my emaciated sister or brother knocking at my door. There's not going to be any osmosis between the two stomachs so that I could transfer some of what I hold to the stomach that is empty. No, it's a matter of changing a relationship. It's ludicrous to think that our "supernatural" charity would be so material—so mechanical as to be reducible to a stomach problem. This would be the very thing with which we've reproached "materialists." If we fail to see the relationship, and see only the bread, clothing, sugar, and coffee, then our *caritas,* however superlatively humanized by great human warmth, and by the cordiality of charitable ladies, won't point to a change in relationship, and will be more materialistic than any political move you ever heard of.

With the gospel in hand, we don't have much choice. We have one option only: an option for those who are the victims of our unlove. But we're lost in the abstractions of idealism. We no longer know who these victims are. Then let us allow the Samaritan, the excommunicated, the outcast, teach us who they are, not theoretically, but in practice. We all know that we should love. We all know that Christian love is not bleating, sentimental humanitarianism, consoling the hearts of just and unjust alike. But when we're asked who our neighbor is, our response is, "Everyone!" In other words, no one.

In his clearest parable—unclear only for those who have no ears to hear—Jesus confronts us with two worlds: the world of the Pharisees—who know perfectly well what they ought to do, and dawdle with the truth, "examining it in depth," turning it this way and that like a veal chop, claiming to want to "clarify" it, but actually adapting it—and the world of praxis, the Samaritan, who knows nothing, has nothing to teach, doesn't know what charity is, and does it.

The neighbor reveals what charity is, identifies it, and shows it to the priest and Levite, if they want to know it and see it. We fly to the last resort, and say: "I have everything in the gospel. I find it all here, the gospel's enough for me. Marxists and atheists don't have anything to teach me. What's all this alms-begging from communists? We're watering down Christian truth, we're burning incense to idols. We should shut ourselves up in our houses and make sure that all our thinking and acting is homemade." But the gospel itself demolishes our excuse, swinging its infallible pickax against all our walls. Jesus might have said: "Who is your neighbor? What kind of question is that? Your neighbor is the next person you meet on the street, the man or woman you meet today when you go to market. Walk out this door and you'll be face to face with your 'neighbor.' She may be a woman driving a Mercedes, or a man with his trousers in tatters and a six-month growth of smelly beard, no matter. Every human being is your neighbor."

Jesus could quote the prophets—who could doubt that he knew them well?—where the neighbor enters the scene in dramatic fashion. But, "no, my friend, you'll learn who your neighbor is from heretics, outcasts. And they'll teach you not with a theory, but with praxis, in an option for help and liberation."

What idealism seeks is not inspired by charity. Its initiatives are not inspired by love for God. They're inspired by hate. It's time to abandon Catholic groups, in outrage. It's 1986 and they're still playing around with the question, "Who are the poor? Who are the oppressed? What will we do if there are no more poor? Close up shop?"

There are ways of learning who the victims of unlove are, if you'd like to know. And the ones who will help you make the identification are the "Samaritans"—the ones who don't want to hear about love any more, but want to actualize it in the world, as they strive for other ideals and other goals.

Religious Deformation

It is in this option that I must live my relationship with God, my relationship of a child to a parent. It is here that I must discover the fatherhood and motherhood that bends solicitously over the lowliest, the least valued, those reckoned as "zeroes"—those who don't exist, in Saint Paul's powerful expression.

A friend of mine with a doctorate in sacred scripture from Rome, doing scholarly work in Jerusalem, an extremely gifted person intellectually, lives in the slums, in love and friendship with his neighbors there. One day a bishop asked him, "What do you talk about with these persons? How can you be interested in their conversation, you who have so much education and training?" The very question strips us, lays our ulcers bare. We are incapable of making a judgment that won't be idealistic. There is no justification for this question in the pretext that leaders have an obligation not to squander their energy, but to use it in the most useful way possible. "Big city slums, the shantytowns, contain enormous numbers of persons deprived of spiritual assistance. What are you doing for their spiritual lives?" My friend answered as he always answers: "I don't know what we talk about, Excellency. I can tell you I'm doing well, and I'm happy." How could he have put into words the exultation of Christ, that leap of joy as Jesus discovered the secrets of the Father revealed to the lowly?

Think a moment how fragile is our discourse on Christ. The diocesan director of religious education can shatter it with a single blow: "Of course the Father has revealed himself to the ignorant, has manifested his secrets to them, has made known to them his inner life. I'll prove it to you in two minutes. Come here, Dolores, stand up straight, don't be shy, tell me, how many gods are there? At what moment does Jesus become present in the bread and wine? There, you see, how wise the simple are? And yet they don't know a word of catechism. . . ."

Jesus' line of reasoning is terribly fragile. It doesn't stand up under the criticism of the ideologues, and we're the ideologues. Had Jesus been present at this oral examination, he would have felt frustrated. What could he have said? "I wanted to say something. But you wouldn't have understood what I had to say, director of religious education, without new eyes, new ears, and a new heart."

If we could read a collection of the verbal and written answers, given by religious superiors and bishops pretty much the world over, to requests from priests and religious to be allowed to go and live among the poor, it would be enough to make us cry. There are some bishops—not the majority, but some—who will not establish a community *except* in a poor neighborhood. But generally the poor are to be visited with love, and frequently, with all possible care and attention, like lepers in a hospital for lepers only. Go there, but don't live there. Help, but don't share. What the bishop who keeps interrogating my friend the doctor of sacred scripture doesn't understand, what the religious education director wouldn't understand, is music on another wavelength, that can be heard only by contemplatives, true contemplatives.

Our professional deformation, our religious deformation, consists in three things: abstractionism (idealism), individualism, and dualism. These are not Christian or "religious" deformations exclusively, but we add the spiritual motivation and "supernatural" justification that makes the disease worse.

Our idealistic training furnishes us with the weapons to destroy all that concrete history presents to us in the way of occasions to love, do justice, and seek communion. After all, what history gives us is impure, ambiguous, ambivalent. We prefer the chemically pure, the abstract. How much evil has been done, and continues to be done, by our mental habit of seeing not human beings, but humanity, *humanitas*—not the poor, but poverty, not a re-created, remade relationship, but celibacy, not a liberating relationship, but obedience, not concrete liberation, but a definition of freedom! We've reduced everything contingent and visible to universal, eternal categories. Now we can catalogue it; we can use it to understand the world of other eras; we can use it to transcend the fleeting tinsel of the apparent and gaze upon what lies beyond. The reduction has infected us with a habit and attitude that we have transmitted to others, the less philosophical. And it has dried up our religious life.

We become terribly concrete and meticulous in economic and organizational matters—wherever our worldly being, the defense of our space or our group's space, is concerned. Our efficiency is frequently the envy of business executives. This sister has her feet on the ground! She knows what it's all about! Behind closed doors, this admiration often becomes scandal. If I did what this sister does with her account books, I'd be in jail, or at any rate fired from my job. When we get right down to it, even what we think of as very practical and concrete is being looked at in an abstract, ideological way. Long have I reflected on this phenomenon. The mercantilism of certain religious is colossal. You have to wear an oxygen mask around them. When "property rights" are dug up out of their bed of abstraction, thrown out in the street, and referred to concrete human relationships, we see the consequences in terms of a social class condemned to malnutrition, underdevelopment, illiteracy, prostitution, and the ravages of alcoholism.

In the abstract, I have the right to build a retreat house on this hill, complete with air conditioning, and a marvelous loudspeaker system that would bring a Jesuit's sermon to a retreatant who wakes up with a liver indisposition, but not so raucously that it will disturb the retreat silence. I could plant a garden all around the house and keep it continuously watered. I could have a swimming pool for retreatants and employees, but of course I'd keep the mangy neighborhood kids out of it. I could put a cyclone fence around my property, with a gate where I can check on who comes in and goes out. But if I get right down to the concrete, and ask myself who my neighbor is, and I see Samaritans going around the neighborhood organizing a hunger march, and I hear women beating their empty water containers and calling me "brother" or "sister" and asking for "water, water, water!"—then I see that this retreat house is *diabolical,* despite all Roman and non-Roman blessings and the good that is done within its walls. It is diabolical in the etymological sense—it sows division, not oneness. It is the instrument of discord, not peace.

Who Is My Neighbor?

Abstraction and ideology can become astutely practical *without facing reality.* And so, to return to the nuns' and priests' construction and banking business, I'd say they're practical, yes, but that they *don't* have their feet on the ground. Theirs is the practicality of the shyster, who knows how to manage the articles of the legal code perfectly to get out of a scrape and win the case, but who has no eyes to see who the defeated are, or what the consequences of his pettifoggery are for them.

I don't have to answer the question "Who is my neighbor?" If I ask myself the question and give myself the answer, I may deceive myself again and again. So, "Ask someone else." And maybe you will be told in terms of the constitutions of a religious congregation, and everything will be crystal clear, and so heartening! And you will be at peace. You will be justified. Sister, your neighbor is the one banging the empty water container, making the noise that reaches your ladylike ears as you wander among the roses, lilies, rhododendrons, all at peace, wrapped in the music of Bach and lulled by the psalms. *This is your neighbor*—the one who begs you for water a few yards from the enclosure where your flowers, the ones you put in front of your Jesus, are forever watered by pipes that never run dry. *This is your neighbor.*

At least have the courage to say what some of the residents of the east side of Caracas say: "I have nothing in common with those people." Perhaps that blasphemy will be the beginning of your redemption. At least the gangsters that live in elegant neighborhoods teach their children that the poor are good-for-nothing drunkards, dishonest persons that you have to look out for, and they train tomorrow's gladiators consciously. Have the stomach and the insensitivity to say that the container-banging is a children's game, and admit the hypocrisy of your sigh: "Ah, you poor people, you are right; water is so necessary—but let me explain to you how far you are from the kingdom of God." No, your real place is with them. You can keep your religious habit or dress as they do, but *go.*

We're sick with dualism. Dualism allows us to move about with disinvolvement in the sphere of idealism or abstraction. This dualism enables us to draw the line, altogether logically, between the secular and the sacred or the "religious." One is here, the other is there, and the separation justifies a life inside the walls, right next to the shacks in which my so-called brothers and sisters live. Dualism justifies my privileges, defines my rights, and keeps everyone in their place. Above all, it furnishes me with the opportunity to take and live the vow of poverty in abundance and security.

It never occurs to us that neither Jesus nor his audience had the cultural support we have for dividing soul from body, for permitting the soul to live the "virtue" of poverty and the body to escape the fears and uncertainties of tomorrow. An Israelite of Jesus' time is not a Greek, and after hearing our disquisitions on poverty, would answer, "What on earth are you talking about?" Why all this talk about poverty of spirit, what it means, what significance it has? It seems to me that it would be enough to consider that in an Israelitic context no one would understand the poverty of something called "spirit" and the wealth of something called "body," because the two of them were unknown in the first place. We meet them in Plato's *Republic.* Here is where they began to fight for their identity.

How shall we attain to Jesus' admiration for the simple if we set up, between them and ourselves, a religious "dignity" modeled so carefully on a bourgeois image? Lest we be pessimistic, we must recognize that there are now more and more priests and religious in the long lines of those beating their ladles against their empty water containers. And the terrible scandal their presence arouses in Latin

America is a double sign: that religion has hitherto had nothing to do with the struggle for justice, and that this new presence of theirs is an efficacious one.

The third wound that we bear on our body is that of individualism: God and I, I and God. It's perfectly true that we begin to have faith when we receive an ultrapersonal message from God, when the Father manifests himself as *my* Father, in the particulars of *my* life. Our relationship with God is a gradual advance in this discovery. But the discovery that God is my Father is part of a wider revelation that all creation is a gift of this Father and that others are my family. My gradual advance in a relationship with my Father proceeds from a strangeness and hostility to an acceptance, from a fear of others, from what Freud calls the "indefinite other," to acceptance, as I see all things, cold and heat, fire and water, stars and humans, as sisters and brothers who accept me and are my friends. The Father has prepared this friendship, and made his steadfast love for us warm, human, sensitive, and near.

Saint John of the Cross has described his terrible climb up the icy wall to reach the pinnacle inaccessible to human beings—to reach "pure act," that burning solitude where one must simply remove one's shoes and adore. But when he reaches the top, he finds fields of flowers, deer, and brooks, making his sojourn delightful. Then he rediscovers painful solidarity with the men and women of his time and history. He returns to his "brothers," who let him languish in prison in Toledo, and there in his cell he rediscovers what an exhilarating yet painful, miserable yet sublime, adventure it is to build communion where none exists.

Communion is either a desire, an aspiration, or else a declamation. When a so-called search for communion ends in "solitude"— that is, in a person's gradual withdrawal from the company of fellow human beings, a gradual withdrawal from the great adventure of communion—doubts arise as to whether the God thus discovered is really the God of Jesus, who is glorified only by our quest for unity. Contemplation is not anesthesia, imperturbability, deliverance from all that might agitate a person, an ascent to the Sea of Tranquility. Jesus' contemplation is defined by his exultation at the sight of beauty and lowliness, and by the groan of Gethsemane. The Christian contemplative is a person gradually immersed in the world's sorrow and assuming that sorrow in his or her flesh and life. To build communion is and will always be the human being's great and terrible cross. "What a wretched man I am! Who can free me from this body under the power of death? . . . All praise to God, through Jesus Christ our Lord!" (Rom. 7:24–25).

Vatican II proclaimed the church of the poor. And this church will come. But we have not understood, and we babble our way through our congresses and our meetings asking what "church of the poor" means. We have failed to understand, and this is a grave matter. Francis of Assisi did not understand the message, "Restore my church." How could he, a lay person, understand that the Lord was asking him for something more than the work of a stone-mason, which he had never done, asking him for something that was "right up his alley"? Restore my church: the church of the poor.

And who are the poor? The poor in faith, the poor in existential motivation, the poor in hope, the poor in love, the physically and psychologically handicapped? It may not be our task, as individual Christians, to catalogue them. Our Father's house has many mansions, and not all of them are occupied by those baptized with water and inscribed on parish registers. Our task, more than in other ages, is to be watchful and available. When and where those identified as the poor "build the church" and are the church, with all the ambiguities and obscurities that will always accompany the various epiphanies of church, we cannot very well know. But we can recognize and admire the love that has always chosen "those whom the world considers absurd to shame the wise . . . the weak of this world to shame the strong . . . the lowborn and despised, those who count for nothing, to reduce to nothing those who were something" (1 Cor. 1:27–28).

The Christian view is surely more profound than the purely political view. In the Christian view, political praxis is not enough, because it leaves *other* poor out of account. But this breadth of vision should not exclude those whom political praxis discovers as poor. Escaping one exclusion, we would fall into a worse exclusion—and be cut off from a wealth of knowledge and support on the part of scientific experience that could afford us irreplaceable aids for recognizing others as excluded.

In the evangelical dismantling of the fraudulent humility in us

Pharisees, we are regenerated and made new human beings, and finally we are liberated from the leaven of the Pharisees. And as new human beings we shall be able to express ourselves in Jesus' song of gladness and hope: "I thank you, Father, for revealing all this to the lowly and the simple."